THE POOP DIARIES

ABBY ROSS

Black Rose Writing | Texas

Third printing

This is a work of non-fiction. Names, characters, businesses, places, events, and incidents are the products of the author's interviews with plumbers across North America. For anonymity purposes, some of the names, and the physical descriptions of homes and people are fictitious.

ISBN: 978-1-68433-426-1
PUBLISHED BY BLACK ROSE WRITING
www.blackrosewriting.com

Printed in the United States of America
Suggested Retail Price (SRP) $18.95

The Poop Diaries is printed in Palatino Linotype

*As a planet-friendly publisher, Black Rose Writing does its best to eliminate unnecessary waste to reduce paper usage and energy costs, while never compromising the reading experience. As a result, the final word count vs. page count may not meet common expectations.

I dedicate this book to all the plumbers who took the time to share their stories with me. Thank you for supporting this project and for the hard work you do to give us life's essentials.

I also dedicate this book to my loving husband, Denis, and our two children, Felix and Heller. Thank you for bringing laughter, support, inspiration, and joy into my life every day.

Finally, thank you to my mom for always being my number one fan.

THE POOP DIARIES

"If I would be a young man again and had to decide how to make my living, I would not try to become a scientist or scholar or teacher. I would rather choose to be a plumber or a peddler in hope to find that modest degree of independence still available under present circumstances."

– Albert Einstein,
published in *Forbes.com* in 2009

INTRODUCTION

One chilly, Wednesday evening in Chicago, I clogged our toilet. My husband suggested we wait until the morning to call a plumber; however, I knew I could not sleep without a working toilet. We moved into our house a few months prior, so we did not have a go-to plumber. After a brief online search, we found Jon. He showed up at 9 p.m. that night, cheery and unexpectedly chatty.

I embarrassingly lingered outside our bathroom door as Jon got to work. He rodded the toilet and convinced us to purchase a new one. The entire job took thirty minutes, yet Jon did not seem to want to leave. He leaned against our kitchen island, chatting away about anything and everything. He was such a nice guy. I did not want to push him out. It was also useful to have a plumber in my back pocket. After ten minutes of chatting, I embraced his extroverted personality and asked him to share his best plumbing stories. What came out of his mouth was so hilarious I felt compelled to write a book.

That is how "The Poop Diaries" was born. After interviewing Jon, I set out to find other plumbers. I asked each one about the most interesting (and sometimes craziest) people they have met, most memorable surprises they have found, and any other "greatest hit" stories that were disgusting, hilarious or scary.

You may assume this book is all about poop, and rightfully, so. When most people think about plumbers, including me, they envision poop. This book, however, is about poop and so much more. Dildos, snakes, rats, fake vaginas, hauntings, weapons, boobs, cheaters, shower obsessions, and drugs are only some examples of what these plumbers have encountered.

I hope you enjoy reading their diaries.

CHAPTER 1
JON

With thirty years of plumbing under my belt, I have seen it all.

I began working in plumbing when I was 13-years-old. A neighbor asked me to join him on jobs. Instead of money, he paid me with free hot dogs and fries, which for most teenagers, was better than money. I attended a few colleges but did not graduate. I am not that good looking, so modeling was off the table. I was in the Navy for five years and was a professional lifeguard, but neither of those jobs paid the bills. So, plumbing was my best option. It paid the bills and made me get my head out of my butt (no pun intended).

If you think plumbing is only about poop, you are wrong. I have seen people during their most vulnerable, naked (literally), and embarrassing moments. I have rescued people from showers, pulled snakes from pipes, and gone head to head with an army of rats. When I go on jobs, I skip peeling back the onion. From the rich to the poor, famous to the everyday "Joe," black, white,

Indian, Asian, every color and culture out there, I see people for who they really are, inside and out.

I am Jon, and these are my diaries.

THE COSMO MODEL

On a sunny day in Chicago, a woman called me.

"My basement is covered in poop," she said. "Please, can you come soon?"

"Sure. No problem, ma'am. I will be right over," I replied.

Those kinds of jobs were run of the mill for me. I went to her house and knocked on the door.

"Hi. I am Jon," I said.

"Hi. I am Amy," she replied, opening the door and gesturing for me to come inside.

Whenever I meet a new customer, I like to make small talk to break the ice, especially because the situation tends to be personal.

"So, what do you do for a living?" I asked.

"I used to be a model. Now, I am a mom," she said.

She must have repeated the model part at least five times during the following five minutes, telling me stories about her modeling days, etc. etc. etc.

I assumed the poop in her basement would be an easy problem to solve, like a backed-up toilet that overflowed, nothing I had not seen before.

I was wrong. It turned out, her sewer had been backed up for weeks, to the point where layers upon layers of feces were caked on the floor, walls, and everywhere else. And it was not all from humans. She had dogs, which she never let outside and cats that forgot how to use a litter box if there was one. Kids' clothes were piled up everywhere, also covered in feces. She did not remove anything from the basement, allowing poop to cover it all, like chocolate frosting on a cake.

I spent hours on my hands and knees, scraping off the poop so I could access the sewer. She hovered over me, yapping and yapping, sharing more stories about her modeling days as if I gave a shit. Finally, I scraped away the poop, found the sewer and unclogged it. Trying to escape quickly, I found the closest table, hunkered down and wrote up the paperwork. My eyes remained focused on the paper, which I hoped would show her I did not want to talk anymore. Then, things got weird.

After filling everything out, I turned around to ask her to confirm the information on the bill was accurate. She was standing over me, stark naked. My eyeballs were almost touching her nipples. I froze, not sure how to proceed.

You may be thinking, "C'mon man! A former model is standing in front of you, naked! Do something! Seize the day!"

Moments prior, I scraped layers of her shit off the floor. I imagined her naked body covered in hard, brown poop, like a statue that stunk.

She continued standing there, unbothered, waiting for me to confirm her information on the bill was accurate. A part of me wondered if she forgot she removed her clothes. A minute later, I snapped out of it.

"Uh, hello?" I said, gesturing my hands up and down to clearly show I was uncomfortable.

"What?" she asked nonchalantly as if standing in front of plumbers naked was a thing she did all the time.

"Lady, please cover-up." I blurted out, relieved I finally said something.

She looked up and down her naked body, giggling. I was clearly the only uncomfortable person in the room.

"Oh, sorry. I am used to being naked from my modeling days," she explained casually. I cringed at the word "modeling." Enough was enough.

She put her clothes back on, signed the paperwork, and walked me out.

Believe it or not, customers – men and women – stripping in front of plumbers is not a novelty. My buddy, who is a very good-looking guy, has been on a few calls where he finished the job, went to his truck to drop off his tools, and headed back inside with the bill only to find customers standing in front of him, naked.

"Add it to my bill," they would say.

One time, I went on a seemingly ordinary call that ended up far from ordinary.

The woman's kitchen sink was broken. While I was shoulder deep inside the cabinet fixing the pipes, she stood over me, staring.

"Want to see something?" she asked. I looked up, without saying anything.

She shoved an entire beer bottle into her mouth, down her throat and back up again to her lips.

"Want to go out Friday?" I blurted out, praying she would accept the invitation.

I had never seen anything like that before. Hell, I wanted to marry her right then and there. We ended up going on a date, just once.

MR. CLEAN
(BUT NOT THAT BALD GUY
YOU ARE THINKING OF)

The strangest call I have ever received has nothing to do with poop.

A woman, who lived in Michigan, called me about her son.

"My son lives in Chicago," she said in a panicky voice. "He has issues and needs help right now."

"Ma'am, we all have issues," I replied, trying to lighten the mood.

"No, seriously," she said, not amused. "He really has issues and needs help."

The urgency in her voice, coupled with her evasiveness made me concerned. My plumbing alias is 'The Plumbing Doctor.'

"Maybe she meant to call a real doctor?" I thought.

"Which day works best for me to stop by his house?" I asked.

"Can you go right now?" she replied, her voice shooting up an octave.

It was 7 a.m.

"What is the urgency?" I asked.

"He needs to go to work, but his shower is broken," she said. "Please, please can you go now?"

I did not understand the problem. Admittedly, although my line of work lends itself to getting dirty, I have gone a day without showering. Although I was not going to argue with the woman. She sounded worried and as a parent myself, I understood that when it came to your children, even the most minor problem was major to you.

She gave me her son's address. He lived in a four-story apartment building that was made of brick. His apartment was on the fourth floor. When I knocked on the door, no one answered. I knocked again, slightly louder.

"Come in!" shouted an echoey voice from inside the apartment. "The door is open."

Alarm bells screamed in my head. What is wrong with this guy? Why won't he answer his own door? Clients always answer their own doors. Many go a step further and look through the peephole first to see who is standing there. Something did not seem right.

"Sir," I said loudly, still standing outside the door. "Please come to the door and let me in."

"I can't," he replied. "Just let yourself in."

I cautiously opened the door, looking for a booby trap or something like it. The apartment was clean and empty. I did not see any signs of a leak, nor smelled feces. The guy was also nowhere in sight. I was confused.

"Where was this guy?" I thought.

Then I remembered his mother said his shower was broken. I headed down a long hallway toward the back of the apartment. Low and behold, I heard a shower running, and he was in it.

The guy was standing in a foot of water, clutching a shower curtain wrapped around his private parts. The shower was still running.

"Sir, please come out of the shower so I can see the problem," I said, trying to hide the frustration in my voice.

"No. I cannot come out. I need to shower and get to work," he replied stubbornly, clutching the curtain a bit tighter.

"Sir, seriously, you need to get out of the shower. Not only is this making me uncomfortable, but I cannot do my job unless I get full access to the shower without you in it," I said, trying not to raise my voice.

He refused.

"I am halfway through my shower. I am not getting out until I finish. You can fix it while I finish," he said.

"Wow," I thought.

He had the nerve to expect me to work around him while he stood there naked, taking a shower.

I threatened to leave unless he got out. He still refused. I tried rationalizing with him, explaining in detail why him being in the shower made it tougher for me to figure out what was wrong. He begged me to stay, yet still refused to get out and would not turn off the shower.

Suddenly, a change of heart struck me. Clearly, this guy had some sort of issue (as his mom said) that disabled him from leaving the shower for ten minutes so I could fix it.

"Okay, I will stay. But please keep that shower curtain wrapped around you and move over slightly," I said. "I do not want your junk on my head."

The guy obliged, relieved he did not have to get out.

I stuck my head inside the shower. At least six cases of soap bars were stacked up on a shelf along the wall. The boxes nearly hit the ceiling. I noticed one of the bars was stuck in the pipe underneath the drain – an easy fix, thankfully. I carefully extended my arm past where the guy was standing, still wrapped in his shower curtain, and popped out the soap. The water drained instantly.

I thought I saw a slight glimpse of "thank you, you are my hero" in the guy's eye until he spoke.

"Please make sure on your way out your tools do not touch my floor, and do not touch the washer and dryer," he said.

"Are you kidding me?" I thought but did not say. Obviously, this guy had much bigger problems than I did that day. At least I fixed one of them. I picked up my tools, glanced at the washer, and dryer on my way out, envisioning my foot slamming into them, restrained myself and left.

EGG DROP SOUP
(SANS THE EGG)

Nothing scares me more than rats. I would rather swim in a basin of diarrhea than stand in a room filled with rats. Poop will not chase me. Poop does not bite. Poop will not give me rabies. My general rule of thumb is if I could potentially bring home a disease, I walk away from the job, which is what almost happened at a Chinese restaurant on the north side of Chicago.

When the owner called, she did not say one word about rats.

"I have an issue," she said. "Can you please come to the restaurant?"

"What is the issue, ma'am?" I asked.

"You will see when you get here," she said.

I agreed to help her, reluctantly. I prefer to know more details about the jobs I agree to do; however, I did not feel like arguing. I had an open day, so I figured I may as well head over there.

When I arrived, the woman was standing outside. She appeared flustered and stressed. Refusing to talk to me anywhere near the dining area, which had about a half dozen customers chomping away on orange chicken and Chow Mein, she silently walked me through the restaurant.

At first, I did not smell anything outside the norm. The Chinese restaurant smell is always pungent, overshadowing all other odors in the room. The woman brought me to the back of the restaurant and down a narrow, wooden staircase that looked about a hundred-years-old. At the bottom, a plastic sheet hung from the ceiling to the floor, which freaked me out. It looked like a scene out of that television show, "Dexter."

"Is this woman going to kill me?" I thought.

She pulled back the curtain and boom! The smell hit me like five hundred tons of shit bricks. Poop was everywhere, and it was not from humans.

"We have a rat problem," she said, so softly I could barely hear her.

Judging by the amount of feces layering the room, it was more than a problem. It was an infestation. At least forty rats pooped on take-out Styrofoam containers and boxes scattered around the room. I anxiously whipped out my flashlight, terrified they were going to jump out and maul me. I looked for eyes and teeth, bracing myself for the attack.

Giving me a much-needed distraction, an employee came downstairs.

"I need more carry-out containers," he said.

Acting as if the poop magically disappeared, the woman nonchalantly pulled out a few Styrofoam containers. With her bare hand, she briskly wiped away the brown poop pellets and handed the containers to the employee.

"Here," she said. "Take these upstairs."

I stood there frozen, full of judgement and shock. How could she put customers' food inside the same containers that were covered in rat poop? Who does that?

"You know that is a health hazard, right?" I asked.

She did not reply. Her eyes shifted down to the floor.

I was about to walk out and report her to the Chicago Department of Public Health, but a question popped up in my head for which I needed an answer.

"Why did she call a plumber and not pest control?" I thought.

I pointed my flashlight towards the sewer and sure enough, spotted giant holes that were so big I could fit my fist through them. The holes were a welcome mat for rats. I imagined them flashing their pointy teeth, walking through the holes, and into the restaurant.

"Hey, what's up? Beef and peapods tonight?" I pictured them saying.

Snapping out of my trance, I showed the owner the holes.

"See those holes? That is how the rats are getting inside. I need to break open the ground and plug the holes," I explained, assuming she would give me the green light to proceed.

"I do not want to pay for that," she said, to my surprise. "How about I give you food as your payment instead of cash?"

Disgusted, I politely declined.

She called me a couple days later, trying to haggle again. The image of rats pooping on take-out containers haunted me. I declined again.

Despite my deep hatred for rats, I do not turn my back on all rat calls. One time a dog walker called me to fix her sewer. Every day for weeks, she flushed down the toilet doggy bags full of poop. It was not the smartest thing to do. She had seventy feet of piled up sewage comprised of poop-filled doggy bags. I had to break open the sewer to fix it, and when I did, two rats scurried out. I jumped, holding back a scream.

Thankfully, I was not alone on the job. My buddy chased the rats into her yard and killed them with a gardening tool. We then fixed the pipe and backfilled it that same day.

The saddest rat infestation I have witnessed happened to a nice, young couple who just bought a new home. The wife was pregnant. She and her husband bought the house when it was in foreclosure. It looked a hundred-years-old and needed a lot of work. The entire structure was leaning to the side - Chicago's very own Leaning Tower of Pisa.

Their plan was to have the baby, live in the house for a year or two, tear it down and rebuild. Unfortunately, things did not go as planned.

The wife called me because her washing machine was not draining. The water kept seeping out onto the basement floor. A section of the floor was dug out. When I shined my light on it, I saw a hundred pairs of eyes staring back at me. I nearly shit myself right there.

"Uh, ma'am, sorry to say this but you have a really bad rat problem," I said, in a slightly higher-pitched voice.

"Noooo!" she yelled, dropping to her knees.

Tears fell from her face.

Knowing the army of rats may emerge and attack any minute, my body kicked into flight mode, wanting to run out of there. My mind, however, chose to fight. I felt sorry for her.

"Ma'am, I am so sorry. Have you ever noticed one or two rats running around this room?" I asked.

"I have no idea," she uttered, sniffling and rubbing her eyes.

They tore down the house a couple months later.

BATHTUB CRINGE

In my line of work, every day is a learning experience. A couple jobs have taught me lifelong lessons, which I will graciously pass along to you. If you buy an apartment building, make sure to do your due diligence in thoroughly understanding your potential renters. Background checks will not cut it. Interview them on the phone and in person. Take them out for drinks and see how they handle themselves. Talk to their friends and family. Call their employer or a professor if they attend college.

As a party lover and moderate socialite, I am not about to poo-poo partygoers. I have the utmost respect for people seeking a good time. On one hand, there is responsible partying, which I welcome. On the other hand, there is outer space partying, where people drink so much, they truly believe they are on another planet, and they don't stop. I do not love that level of partying, although it does pay my bills.

The outer space partyers are the types of people I usually encounter. And I must say, their creativity in toilet alternatives blows my mind.

On an early Sunday morning, my phone rang.

"Hey, Jon," said one of my regular customers.

He owned an apartment building in the Lincoln Park neighborhood of Chicago.

"Can you stop by one of my three-bedroom units? Five college girls are renting it. They threw a party last night and their toilet seat and tank broke," he explained.

"Sure, no problem," I said. "I will head there now."

These calls never surprise me. They are the typical college campus plumbing stories, although in this case, I saw something I had never seen before.

I arrived at the apartment at 10 a.m. Standing outside the door, I could hear music and people chatting. Clearly, the party had not ended. When I knocked on the door, a twenty-something girl answered.

"Hi. I am Jon, the plumber," I said.

It was pointless to make small talk. Her eyes drooped to her cheeks. Her body hunched over. After partying the night away, it was obvious she was not in the best mindset to discuss what subject she was studying at school.

She opened the door wider, without a saying a word. A waft of shit smell blew into my face. Walking through a trail of beer cans and empty wine bottles, I followed the scent to the bathroom.

The room was small, which made the smell even more dominating. Considering the toilet broke the night before, the communal sewage had been sitting in the tank for a while. The stench was strong, to say the least. It burned my eyes.

Fortunately, the fix was easy. I drained the toilet and replaced it, which took about fifteen minutes. With a new toilet installed, I expected the stink to fade away, but it stayed, as strong as ever. I was perplexed. I just installed a fresh, new toilet. Why did it still smell like shit?

Interrupting my thoughts, one of the girls popped her head in.

"The tub is clogged too," she blurted out, and ran away.

Like most apartment bathrooms, the tub sat next to the toilet. It had an off-white color shower curtain, which was closed. The end of it was tucked inside the tub. I pulled it back.

"Holy shit," I accidentally said out loud.

The tub was filled with at least four inches of pee and poop. Brown nuggets clung to the side. Yellow urine pooled at the bottom. Up until that moment, I had never seen anyone shit in a tub. It was different and disgusting. Fortunately, since I had already spent quite a bit of time with the stink permeating, I was used to the stench.

I called the landlord.

"This is going to cost you extra," I said.

THE COVER GIRL

I am a lucky guy to have magazine models calling me, begging me to come over. I confess most of the time, they only want me to unclog their toilets. It still counts though, and I enjoy it, except for one time. I would have been just fine if I had not taken one model's call.

"Hello," she said. "My toilet is clogged. I need help fixing it."

It seemed like a run-of-the-mill job.

"I will be right over," I said.

Her house was a sprawling two-story white brick home. It had a long driveway that snaked through the front yard. I parked near the end of it and walked up to the front door. When she opened it, my jaw dropped to the floor. My eyes bulged out of their sockets. I had never seen such a gorgeous woman. Her skin was flawless. She had an unforgettable smile and legs that went on for miles. She was phenomenal. I nearly forgot why I was there.

"Hi," I squeaked. "I am Jon, the plumber."

"Follow me. The bathroom is down this hall," she said, snapping me out of my trance.

Framed cover pages of magazines filled the walls of the hallway. Each one featured the gorgeous woman leading me to her bathroom.

"Those photographs are of me," she said matter-of-factly. "I am a model."

My legs felt like they were going to collapse. I needed to snap out of it.

"I am here to unclog her toilet," I thought. "There is nothing sexy about that, but she is so hot!"

The bathroom was at the end of the hallway. It was clean and modern. A white, porcelain sink and vanity stood against the wall. Gray wooden shelves lined the walls. It even had a large shower with a double glass door.

"So," I said, clearing my throat. "Can you explain to me again what is wrong with the toilet?"

"Oh, my toilet," she responded, her cheeks flushing from embarrassment, which I thought was adorable. "It is messy in there."

"No problem. Let me look," I said.

The second I lifted the seat; my encounter with this gorgeous woman quickly went south. The bowl was so abominable, I instantly vomited into it. I will spare you the revolting details (like chunks of fava beans) but to give you an idea, I have only vomited on a job three times in three decades. This was one of them.

She was mortified. I saw her from the corner of my eye, slowly stepping backward out of the bathroom. Feeling bad about my reaction, I wanted to make her feel better. I never want to embarrass people.

"Don't worry!" I thought about saying. "I vomit all the time on jobs. It is par for the course!"

I did not say any of those things. My eyes were burning so badly, I could not get a word out.

Half blinded, I quickly used my air ram tool to clear the toilet. She walked away, leaving me alone to finish the job.

Her toilet set the record for the worst clogged bowl I had seen up until that point. Little did I know that record was about to be broken.

SIXTEEN YANKEE CANDLES

The call seemed like every other call.

"My toilet is clogged," said the woman. "I need you to come over and fix it as soon as possible."

"Sure, ma'am," I replied. "I will be there soon."

She lived on the tenth floor of a modern high rise in downtown Chicago. When I arrived, she opened the door.

"Hi. I am Jon, the plumber," I said. "I am here to fix the toilet."

The woman had grayish-brown, shoulder-length hair. She was wearing reading glasses with a chain connected to them.

"Come in," she said, pushing the glasses down to the tip of her nose to get a better look at me.

Her apartment was clean. It had dark wood floors and light gray walls. She walked me past the open living room, dining area, and kitchen, and into the master bedroom, which connected to the bathroom.

"This is the clogged toilet," she said.

Surprisingly, the bathroom smelled kind of nice. Big, purple, Yankee candles were scattered everywhere – inside the bathtub, above the sink, and on the toilet tank. It looked like she lit them hours ago because soot stuck to the ceiling. Air fresheners sat in every corner of the room. Clearly, she had something to hide.

Once my eyes adjusted to all the purple, I walked over to the toilet and lifted the seat. Without hesitation, I threw up in the bowl.

Dried, crusty poop was packed to the brim. The smell of pepper and curry permeated the air. My eyes felt like they were on fire.

"How long have you been without a toilet?" I asked, coughing repeatedly.

"Three weeks," she said.

"Three weeks! Why three weeks?" I asked.

"I thought the longer I waited, the less expensive it would be," she explained. "And I was embarrassed."

Her face flushed.

The first part of her explanation made no sense whatsoever, but I understood the latter part. Embarrassment is a natural reaction for my clients, and in this case, especially, I could see why.

I shoved my air ram into the bowl. The poop was so hard it felt like I was pushing through a boulder of dried mud. The smell was abhorrent. I tried holding my breath. My eyes would not stop watering. No matter what I did, I could not escape the scent of curry, pepper, and shit. The candles topped off everything, like the cherry on a shit sundae. The purple haze and lavender smell only added to my nausea.

The job was pure torture. It took me thirty minutes to scoop out the poop and get the toilet to work again. The moment I finished, I stuck my head out the doorway, gasping for clean, non-lavender-curry-pepper-shit smelling air.

The woman watched me. Her face was bright red.

"Will you clean the bowl for me too?" she asked, almost in a whisper as she looked down at the floor.

"Clean the bowl? I am a plumber, lady! I do not clean toilets!" I thought.

"No," I politely replied and left.

I HAVE HAD IT WITH THESE MOTHA**#*** SNAKES IN THESE MOTHA**#*** DRAINS!

One job takes the cake for the weirdest thing I have ever found clogging a line. On a summer day in Chicago, one of my regular customers called asking for help. He owned an old apartment building downtown. Three tenants, who lived in a two-bedroom unit, had a backed-up sink.

Within the hour, I went to the apartment, drained the sink, ran the water to make sure it did not back up again and left. I called the building owner after I finished the job.

"It is done," I said. "The sink is unplugged and working."

"Thank you so much, Jon," he replied.

Two weeks later, he called again.

"The sink is backed up again," he said. "I do not know what the problem is or what they are putting down there, but I need you to fix it."

He then dropped his voice to a low, muffled tone.

"One of my tenants said you have no idea what you are doing and asked me to hire another plumber," he murmured.

"What?!" I exclaimed. "The nerve! I know I fixed that sink!"

My face flushed with anger. I hate when people do not trust me. I knew I fixed their sink. I tested it. It worked. Plumbing is not rocket science, despite what people may think. There are only so many things that can go wrong on just a few things – sinks, tubs, and toilets. If the tub is clogged, you unclog it. First, rod it. If that does not work, use an air ram, jet or pistol rod. If the toilet is leaking, find out why. It is either a broken toilet, seal or pipe. Whichever one it is, replace it.

If plumbing were rocket science, I would not be doing it.

Fortunately, in this case, the owner and I had a rapport. He trusted me. I went back that day and brought a couple guys with me. The tenants were not home. We did the exact same thing as I did the last time, however, unlike last time, the sink would not drain.

"Did the tenants do something to it? What changed?" I said.

We stood there, perplexed. I tried rodding it again. We worked on it for a couple hours to no avail. I called the building owner.

"We need to remove the pipes and clean them out," I explained. "It will cost you more money because it is a more time-consuming job. I need to figure out what changed between two weeks ago and today."

"Do you really have to?" he asked.

"Sorry, man. We have been working on this for hours, and I cannot get it open," I said.

"Oh, okay," he said, sounding disappointed.

I felt bad for the guy. He was not expecting a higher price; however, we were also not expecting additional labor.

My colleague cut up a section of the pipe. He then took a grinder to the next section.

To my surprise, within seconds, he threw up all over the floor. Our other colleague walked over, took a whiff inside the pipe, and ran out with a mouthful of vomit.

"What is going on?" I thought. "We rarely vomit on jobs."

And then the smell hit me. Out of all the toilets I have unclogged, all the poop, vomit and every other bodily fluid I have smelled, this stench was the worst. It smelled like death. It was a rancid, acidic, rotten fish egg-like stench. Within minutes, it infiltrated the whole unit. Our eyes were burning. We could not breathe. Our stomachs turned over and over. We frantically opened the windows and ran out.

Standing outside the building, we looked up at the apartment window, wondering what the hell emitted that horrific smell. We stood there for two and a half hours, calming our stomachs and waiting for the place to air out.

Committed to finishing the job, we went back inside. My colleague cautiously approached the pipe and stuck his hand inside. To our gruesome surprise, he pulled out a six-foot-long snake and two dead mice. It was disgusting. The snake was in pieces. We could see the greenish, brownish, yellowish skin. It must have eaten the mice, crawled into the kitchen line and drowned. I could not wrap my head around how the six-foot-long snake squeezed into the two-inch-long line, let alone with two rats in its stomach. I was not a genius with numbers, but I knew that math did not add up.

I did not have the time nor the stomach to hypothesize. The smell and sight were so disgusting, my legs moved faster than my brain, making a beeline towards the door. Although I did not get very far.

"This owner is a regular customer," I thought. "He trusted me when his tenant doubted me. I had to stay and get the job done."

My brain prevailed. I walked back inside to finish the job.

Because of the smell, we could only work in twenty-minute intervals. The job took about an hour to finish. Minutes before we headed out, one of the tenants came home. She looked to be in her twenties with long blond hair and a pale complexion. I assumed she was the one who doubted my work because she did not even acknowledge my presence. She walked straight past me, like I was a ghost, and approached one of my colleagues. I admit he was much better looking.

"Yeah, I lost my snake about two weeks ago," I overheard her say.

"What kind of snake?" replied my colleague.

"It was about six-feet-long," she said.

"Really?" said my colleague.

"Yeah. Sometimes I let it out. But it always came back. It will come back," she said.

We did not have the heart to tell her otherwise. We also did not want her to think we killed it. Based on the smell, that snake had died well before our arrival. Nonetheless, people love to point fingers, and she did not trust me to begin with, so it was best not to say anything. We told the building owner. He did not take the news well.

"What?!" he exclaimed. I could hear the anger in his voice.

"Pets are not allowed in the building! The rules are spelled out in the lease!" he said.

He told the tenant about the snake and demanded she pay our bill.

I have found kittens in sewers, rats in all kinds of places, and even a squirrel one time. That day was the first (and hopefully last) time I had ever found a snake.

A MOMENT OF REFLECTION

The best and sometimes worst part about my job is that there is always a surprise. While the unexpected may be horrifically disgusting, at least it is unexpected, which keeps things interesting.

I would like to pass on some words of wisdom. Do not think you know or have seen it all. People will always surprise you. I enjoy meeting every one of them, no matter how pleasant, disgusting, or awkward the encounter. Sometimes I meet people who are too trusting and overly nice. Other times, I meet people who do not trust me at all. Some people are extremely smart and could easily fix the problem themselves if they wanted to fix it. Others, I am surprised can even open the door to get out of their house.

People surprise me in all kinds of situations, yet I find a way to treat everyone equally, with the same level of respect. That is part of the job, and it is one I do not plan on leaving any time soon.

CHAPTER 2
CARISSA

I used to manage a bunch of apartment buildings with my grandma. She exposed me to every facet of the business such as getting loans from banks, showing apartments to tenants, evictions, carpentry, painting, and plumbing. You name it; I did it. My grandma taught me how to do everything. I worked with her for nine years, until I was twenty-six-years-old. At that point, I wanted a change. My aunt, mom, and uncle took over my part of the business, giving me the opportunity to do my own thing.

I liked any job that involved working with my hands, so I started with carpentry. I enjoyed it but learned that when carpenters move up the ladder, they run job sites. They are the first person on-site in the morning and the last person to leave in the evening. They become general contractors and must babysit the electricians, plumbers and other trades. Trying to get all the guys to listen to me was not my cup of tea. I am a woman in a male-dominated industry, which makes everything more challenging.

One time I was leading a job at a customer's home. One of the carpenters, who I was managing, was tasked to install granite countertops. He parked his truck in the driveway so he could easily carry the granite into the house. When he was working on the installation, however, I received a call from the window guys. They needed to install a big bay window and asked if the carpenter could move his truck so they could park close to the house.

"Hey Bill," I said. "Can you please move your truck so the window guys can park there? They have a big bay window they need to bring inside."

He completely ignored me, pretending not to hear me. The job site was quiet that morning. It was nearly impossible for him not to have heard me.

"Bill," I repeated. "Can you please move your truck? The window guys need to park there."

"You need to use your big boy voice," he snapped, without even glancing in my direction.

After a comment like that, I was no longer playing nicely.

"You need to move your stupid, fucking truck right fucking now or you will never work at one of my job sites ever again!" I yelled.

He looked at me. I stared back at him, with daggers sticking out of my eyes. He walked out in a huff and moved his truck.

That incident was the straw that broke the camel's back. I had enough with carpentry. After taking a long, hard look at my options, I decided to go to plumbing school. Plumbers will always have work, even in a bad economy. When money is tight, people will always find a way to pay for a plumber because they need hot and running water and a working toilet. I had also never been an office kind of person. I wanted to go somewhere and do something different every day. Not to mention, in Canada, the first two years of plumbing school focus on pipe and steam fittings. The last two years focus on a plumbing specialization. So, when you graduate, you have a broad skill set and a range of options, some of which have nothing to do with poop. I have worked on geothermal systems, boilers, floor heating systems, and gas lines. I installed paint lines in newspaper printing machines and paint booths for cars. A plumber is required for pretty much anything that has to do with a pipe.

I have been a plumber for the past eight years and have zero regrets. I meet all sorts of interesting people and go to all sorts of interesting places.

I am Carissa, and these are my diaries.

DUDE, REALLY?

Being a service plumber, I have worked for a few companies that have required an on-call shift. One week each month, I carried an on-call phone. If a customer called, I had to arrive at the house or wherever the problem was within one hour. If more than one person called during the same window of time, the boss would have to wake up and go, which did not happen often.

During one of those on-call weeks, at half-past midnight, the phone woke me up from a deep slumber. It was from a waitress at a bar.

"The mainline in the men's washroom is plugged," she said. "Nothing is working, and this place is packed. Can you please come fix it?"

"Alright. I will be right over," I replied, still half asleep.

Since I had to arrive at the bar within one hour, I could not afford to move slowly. I jumped out of bed, threw on a t-shirt, light brown coveralls, and a sweater jacket, and headed to my plumbing van.

The bar was a long, brick building with big windows on each side. Cars filled every space in the front parking lot, so I parked in the back by the entrance to the kitchen. I pressed the delivery buzzer outside the kitchen door. A dishwasher greeted me.

"Hi, I am the plumber," I said.

"Come in," he replied, opening the door wider.

The kitchen was loud and hot. People were everywhere, yelling out orders, clanking pots and pans and washing dishes. I climbed a staircase that led to an office. The manager and waitress who had called me were chatting inside. They looked up when they saw me in the doorway.

"Hello!" they said in unison, seemingly overjoyed to see me.

"Thank you for coming so quickly," said the manager.

"No problem. Can you show me the washroom?" I asked.

He walked me downstairs through the packed bar and into the men's washroom.

"A group of guys were in here earlier; however nothing was working. Be careful. Sometimes we find needles and stuff in the toilets," he said and walked away.

The bathroom was large. Eight toilet stalls were on the right side of the room, backed up against the beige, tile wall. Twelve urinals were on the left, closer to the door. A row of sinks stood in front of the toilets. For the most part, the bathroom was clean, except for the area around the floor drain, which sat in the middle of the toilets and urinals. Shit, toilet paper, and vomit oozed out of the drain. When you work in bar bathrooms, you find a mix of odd and disgusting stuff clogging the lines. Whatever someone wore on their head while leaning over to puke in the toilet – costume jewelry, sunglasses, headbands with feathers – we find it.

The pile of excrement, as disgusting as it sounds, did not bother me. The smell did not nauseate me either. My family lived on a farm. Growing up, I frequently smelled rotten wheat, which is a million times worse than the smell of feces. One of my chores was to empty the wheat bin and take it to the grain pool. Some of the grain would stick to the bottom of the bin and become rotten and mushy. Mice and rats crawled in for a taste and often wound up dying. By the time I emptied the bin, their corpses were rotted along with the grain. I had to shovel it out to make room for more. It was the most horrific smell in the world. The experience gave me the gift of a strong stomach, a gift that comes in handy for a plumber.

I placed an "Out of Service" sign on the bathroom door and got to work. To avoid sticking my snake down the filthy floor drain, I looked for the cleanout, which was at the end of the bathroom. It only took a few minutes to unclog everything; however my job was not finished. I noticed a urinal was not draining properly, so I pulled it off the wall and stuck the snake down there as well. It quickly unplugged. Suddenly, I heard a guy's voice behind me.

"Oh, sorry," he stammered nervously.

I turned around. The guy looked to be about my age – thirty years old. He had short, brown hair and a medium size build. He was noticeably drunk, although it was 1:30 a.m. in a bar, so that was to be expected.

"It is okay," I said. "I am almost finished."

"The other washroom is full, so I thought I would use this one," he replied.

"Well if you are not shy, feel free to use a urinal," I said, glancing at the row of urinals.

While he stood there, deciding which one to use, I picked up the urinal I had unplugged and began reinstalling it against the wall. Out of the eleven urinals to choose from, the guy chose to pee in the one directly next to me. Fortunately, there were stall-like dividers on the sides of the urinals so I could not see anything, although I heard it. The sound of pee slapping against porcelain echoed through the bathroom. I tried to ignore it, focusing on tightening the urinal against the wall.

"So, are you single?" he asked, in mid-stream. "Want to go out sometime?"

Laughing hysterically, I nearly dropped the urinal.

"Are you seriously asking me out right now? You cannot wait until you finish peeing?" I asked incredulously.

He stopped peeing.

"Oh sorry," he stammered again, clearly embarrassed. "So, that is a *no* then?"

I could not stop laughing.

"Can I at least peek around and see if I want to say 'yes?'" I asked half-joking.

"No," he said curtly.

He quickly zipped up his pants and ran out of the washroom. He did not even wash his hands. I finished the job, removed the sign from the washroom, and walked back through the bar to find the manager. I never saw that guy again.

THE BATHROOM SADIST

The first time a guy asked me out at a job site was when I was a first-year apprentice. I will never forget that day. I was assigned to unclog a drain in the women's washroom of a large, commercial building. Three hundred employees worked there. The building stretched across an entire block with large parking lots on both sides. The job was my first one that day. It is never fun to work on washroom drains first thing in the morning. You spend the entire day dirty and stinky.

I arrived at the building at 8:30 a.m. The receptionist greeted me.

"Hi, I am the plumber. I am here to fix the drain in the women's washroom," I said. "Can you please introduce me to the maintenance guy? He needs to show me the bathroom."

Five minutes later, the maintenance guy walked through the doors. He was an older gentleman. His head was totally bald. He wore a blue maintenance uniform.

"Hello there," he said with a smile. "How is your day going?"

"Good," I replied, smiling back. "It is early though. How is your day going?"

"Great!" he exclaimed.

We walked down a long hallway, passing the main office, which was filled with desks and cubicles. We walked past one set of washrooms, which were working fine. Looking up and around, I checked out all the plumbing as we continued walking. Sometimes I need all the information I can get before I start a project. We walked through a set of double doors, across a warehouse and towards the back, until we reached the second set of washrooms.

"Here we are," he said, opening the women's washroom door.

The bathroom was large. It had five, dark green stalls and bright white walls. Poop and toilet paper covered the white, tile floor. The sewage backed up about three feet to the floor drain. The water was continuously running on one of the toilets, causing the water to overflow and spillover. The room smelled like pure sewage. Sometimes when I work in bathrooms, they smell like perfume spray on top of poop. In this case, however, it only smelled like poop, which frankly I prefer over perfume covered poop.

"I have to get more tools," I said to the maintenance guy.

My snake would not be enough. The place needed a light clean when I was finished.

"Walk through the warehouse to the secretary's desk who can point you to the parking lot," he said.

"Thanks," I replied.

I went back to my van, collected more tools and cleaning supplies, and headed back inside. While walking towards the first set of washrooms, I saw a guy leaning against the wall, watching me. He looked young and was tall. He had long hair, which hung over his ears. He wore light jeans and a t-shirt with a rock band logo on it.

"Hello," he said as I walked by him.

"Hi," I replied, and kept walking.

He started walking with me.

"I have not seen you around before," he said. "Why are you here?"

"I do not work here," I replied, staring straight ahead. "I am here to fix the plumbing."

"Oh yeah? What is broken?" he asked.

When we arrived at the double doors, he held one open for me.

"The women's washroom is plugged," I said. "I have to unplug it."

"What company do you work for?" he asked.

I hesitated, not knowing if I should disclose my company's name. Although considering my branded van was parked in the lot, I told him.

When we reached the women's washroom, I stopped and looked up at him.

"Okay," he said, catching my hint. "I will let you get to work."

Inside the washroom, I took a deep breath. Among the shit, toilet paper, and smell of sewage, I started to relax.

The job was easy. The minute I stuck my snake down the floor drain, everything unplugged. The water started draining, leaving nuggets of poop and toilet paper behind. I dumped a bucket of water down the drain to eliminate the smell, cleaned up the poop and toilet paper, and dried the floor with a rag pinned under my shoe. The broken toilet was still running. To fix it, I had to install a new flapper. The part was in my van. With my snake in hand, I walked out of the washroom. Surprisingly, the guy was waiting for me. He must have stood there for the entire hour I was working.

"How did it go?" he asked.

I paused, not knowing how to respond. It was such an odd question.

"Can I help you with anything? Can I carry that?" he asked, pointing to the coils that came with my snake.

"No, thank you," I said. "I am okay."

I walked quickly towards the warehouse.

"Did you get everything fixed up?" he asked, following my every step.

"Almost," I said. "What do you do here?"

It seemed unusual that he had the free time to hang around outside a washroom for an hour. I thought (and hoped) he was the maintenance man's assistant or someone connected to plumbing. Why was he still there? Didn't he have a job to do?

"I work in the cubicles up front," he replied.

"Do you need anything? Can I help you?" I asked, coming to a halt outside the first set of washrooms.

"Well, actually," he stammered. "I was wondering if you want to go out sometime?"

"UGH," my inner voice screamed. Now everything made sense. I wanted to let him down gently. He seemed like an awkwardly nice guy.

"That is flattering," I said with a smile. "I am actually seeing someone right now but thank you. You seem like a nice guy."

I was not seeing anyone; however, I was ninety-nine percent certain he had no way of knowing that.

He put his hands in his pockets and shrugged his shoulders. His eyes shifted downwards to the floor.

"Okay, well, I had to try," he murmured. "You never know, right?"

He looked at me one more time, turned around, and quickly walked away.

Although he seemed embarrassed, I thought he handled the rejection well. I went back outside to my van, dropped off my snake, and grabbed the flapper.

Within fifteen minutes, I fixed the broken toilet, double-checked that everything was cleaned up and left. On my way out, I saw the maintenance guy.

"All set?" he asked.

"Yes," I said. "Everything is fixed and cleaned up. Do you want to look at it before I leave?"

"Nah, it's okay," he said with a smile. "I am sure you did a great job. I will check it out later."

I waved goodbye and left.

When I arrived at the office the next morning, my boss approached me.

"Hey, Carissa," he said curtly.

His lips were pressed together tightly. I knew something was wrong.

"What is wrong?" I asked nervously.

"Can you come to my office?" he said.

"Okay, sure," I replied, following him to his office.

He sat down at his rectangular, wooden desk. I sat across from him. My hands fidgeted in my lap.

"How did your day go yesterday?" he asked. "Did anything eventful happen?"

"It was fine," I replied, confused. "Nothing happened."

"Are you sure nothing got broken?" he asked.

"I swear I only fixed things yesterday," I said, laughing. When I am nervous, I always laugh.

"Can you walk me through the first job you did that day?" he asked.

I told him about the washroom job, omitting the part about the guy because I did not think it was relevant.

"Are you sure you cleaned up the washroom before you left?" he asked. "You left it cleaner than when you got there?"

"Well considering there was shit on the floor before I got there, that was not hard to do," I joked.

"Oh," he said, looking puzzled.

"Why are you asking me this?" I asked.

"Because apparently the washroom was destroyed," he said.

"DESTROYED?!" I yelled in disbelief.

"There was toilet paper, and poop smeared all over the walls and floor," he explained. "There was a huge hole in the wall, too, like someone threw a toilet into it."

"What!!!???" I exclaimed. "No, absolutely not! How could I put a hole in the wall? My snake was not anywhere near it. It takes heavy lifting to put a giant hole in the wall. I could not do that!"

I was standing up at that point. I could not believe he was accusing me of trashing a bathroom.

"It is okay," he said calmly. "I believe you."

Fortunately, the building had cameras everywhere, including outside the washroom. It turned out the guy, who I rejected, went into the washroom after I left and destroyed it. The footage showed him brazenly storming in and leaving after about ten minutes. I guess he did not take my rejection that well, after all.

When my boss found out about the footage, he called me into his office.

"Carissa, please come in here!" he yelled, snickering.

"What is so funny?" I asked.

He told me the whole story.

"You know," he said. "Please do not take this the wrong way. I like having you as an employee, but I will never get used to having a girl around here. These things just do not happen to the boys."

"Sorry!" I said, chuckling.

"It is okay," he said, chuckling with me.

I left his office feeling relieved. If that guy was crazy enough to trash a bathroom after one rejection, I cannot imagine the pain I would have suffered if I had dated him. It looked like I dodged a major bullet.

THE UNINTENTIONAL HOMEWRECKER

One warm summer day, I was asked to fix a plugged toilet in a home. I arrived in the late afternoon. The house was big, with light yellow siding, and a long driveway. A giant evergreen tree stood in the front yard. My boss instructed me to park on the street because my van had been leaking oil. He did not want it to leak in the customer's driveway. I parked, grabbed some tools, and walked up to the front door.

A middle-aged man greeted me. He had grayish, brown hair – more salt than pepper. He wore dress pants and a white t-shirt.

"Thank you for coming," he said warmly. "Feel free to leave your shoes on."

"It is okay. I will take them off," I said.

Out of courtesy, I always take off my shoes inside customers' homes.

I walked into the entryway foyer. Family photos covered the left side wall. A long hallway extended through the main floor. At the end, I could see the kitchen and a bathroom on the right.

"Is that the bathroom with the plugged toilet?" I asked.

"No. It is the one upstairs," he replied. "I will show you."

He quietly led me upstairs. Except for a soccer ball in the hallway, the house was spotless. It was obvious his wife decorated the master bedroom. A pink, floral pattern adorned the curtains and bedspread. A large, walk-in closet was along the front wall. Women's pants, dress shirts, skirts, and dresses were lined up perfectly on the left side. Men's slacks, sweaters, and collared shirts lined up on the right side. The master bathroom was beautiful. It had a sleek, white jacuzzi tub and a big shower with a bench inside.

"This is the plugged toilet," explained the man, pointing to the white, porcelain toilet. "It happened when my wife was home, so I do not know how it plugged."

"Has the toilet been plugged before, or is this the first time?" I asked.

"I don't know," he said.

Judging by the soccer ball and lack of baby toys laying around, I assumed his children were old enough to know not to put anything, besides toilet paper, down the toilet.

"Do you know if anyone put anything down there besides toilet paper?" I asked, just to double-check.

"I am not sure," he replied. "I will let you get to work. If you need anything, I will be in my office downstairs."

I crouched down to assess the toilet. The man had turned off the water. It drained slowly. The inside of the bowl was clean. It did not even look backed up, although the man insisted it was plugged. I turned on the water and flushed. Sure enough, the water did not go down. It rose rapidly to the top of the bowl.

Armed with my smaller snake, I stuck it down the bowl. The snake only goes about six feet down, which in most cases, does the trick because the plug is usually in the toilet. This time, however, it was unsuccessful. I removed the toilet from the floor, exposing a three-inch pipe. I needed a bigger snake.

"I will be right back!" I yelled to the man as I walked downstairs, out the door and to my van.

I returned with my bigger snake. This one goes one hundred feet down the pipe, and the cable is six times as big. I put the snake down the pipe that stuck out of the floor. Usually, the bigger snake pushes the blockage through, preventing me from seeing it. In this case, however, when I pulled out my snake, a giant wad of condoms came with it. At least twenty condoms, which looked used and brown from the sewage water, stuck to the end of my snake. I felt a little grossed out, being that I had never pulled out such a large pile of used condoms. In a way, it was more disgusting than sewage. I put on an extra pair of rubber gloves to yank them off and throw them away. I then fastened the toilet back into the floor.

The man's voice snuck up behind me.

"Did you fix it?" he asked.

"Yes. It is fixed," I replied.

"What was plugging it?" he asked, smiling.

"I pulled out a giant wad of condoms," I stated. "You cannot flush condoms down the toilet. You should throw them in the garbage."

No matter how embarrassing a situation may be, I always try to educate my customers about what they can and cannot flush down the toilet.

The smile washed off the man's face. He looked as if he suddenly became ill. His face blanched. I assumed he was embarrassed by the situation. After all, a stranger, let alone a female stranger, pulling a wad of your condoms out of your toilet creates the perfect recipe for an awkward moment.

He walked away without saying a word. Feeling sorry for the guy, I packed up my tools and headed out.

"My company will invoice you!" I said loudly as I was leaving.

"Thank you for your work," he replied softly. "Have a nice day."

When I went into work the next morning, my boss was livid. On most days, he greeted me with a smile the minute I walked in the door. That day, however, he stared at me quietly, along with everyone else in the room.

"I need to talk to you in my office now," he murmured through his tightly locked jaw.

I nervously followed him into his office.

"Am I getting fired?" I thought. "No way. I have done good work for this company."

Plumbers must do something catastrophic to get fired, such as flooding a home or blowing up something. I did not do any of those things. Every possible scenario ran through my head. What went wrong with one of my projects?

He sat down behind his large, wooden desk. I sat down in a chair across from him.

"How did your day go yesterday?" he asked.

"It went well. Why?" I asked puzzled.

"Did anything out of the ordinary happen?" he asked.

"No," I stated.

"Please explain to me step-by-step what happened with the plugged toilet job in the late afternoon," he said.

Typically, when the boss asks you to walk through a job, it means an unsatisfied customer called the office. I explained every detail about the job. When I mentioned the wad of condoms, his shoulders noticeably relaxed, and his clenched jaw loosened. A slight smile appeared.

"What is going on? Why are you asking me this?" I asked, confused by the sudden change of expression.

The story that came out of his mouth astonished me. Before I arrived that morning, the salt and pepper-haired man's wife called. She screamed at the receptionist and demanded to talk to my manager. When my boss answered, she continued screaming, to the point of shrieking. She was hysterical.

"Your plumber ruined my marriage! She ruined it!" she shrilled. "You should fire her and be careful who you hire in the future!"

When my boss repeated her words to me, I knew exactly what had happened. The condoms I pulled out did not belong to her husband. Her lover was flushing them down the toilet. The wife got busted because of me. Worse yet, my boss thought I was fucking the husband, which I would never ever do.

I started laughing. The situation was not funny, but I did not know how to react.

"Are you serious?" I asked.

"I am completely serious," he replied. "And, I am sorry."

"It is okay," I said. "I am sorry if I stressed you out. That lady is crazy. I hope you know I would never sleep with a customer."

"I know," he said. "Again, I am sorry."

Once again, I doubt male plumbers face those kinds of situations.

LET'S <u>NOT</u> HUG IT OUT

For whatever reason, people like to hug me. Maybe it is because I am short or because I am a girl. My male plumber colleagues think it is hilarious when people hug me. They know I am not a touchy, feely, hug-loving person. Even when the girls at work hug me, my body tenses. I am only comfortable hugging my family, particularly my sister. For everyone else, I may as well wear a sign that says, "Do not touch."

I wish I had that sign four years ago while walking through a parking lot during my lunch break. My apprentice and I were between jobs. My apprentice was a nice, tall, young guy – around twenty-years-old – and built. He exercised at least four times a week. Typically, when companies pair apprentices with plumbers, they get to know each other very well. The goal is for the apprentice to know exactly how the plumber operates – from where she keeps her tools to how she likes to get jobs done. My apprentice and I worked together every day, so we knew a lot about each other, personally and professionally.

With minimal free time and rumbling stomachs, we pulled into a big parking lot outside a fast food restaurant. Since we were driving our plumbing van, we parked towards the back of the lot, so we could get out easily. It was 2:30 p.m. and I was already tired. The first job that morning drained my energy. Luckily, the parking lot was almost empty, which meant we would not have to stand in a long line at the restaurant. I was wearing my usual work outfit – big, brown coveralls over a navy-blue t-shirt. Women's clothing in the trades has slowly improved over the years. Today, I wear contemporary, black work pants with extra pockets and a built-in tool belt.

My apprentice and I hopped out of the van.

"I am so hungry," I said, as we were walking in the parking lot.

"I know," he replied. "That last job took much longer than expected."

"We only have fifteen minutes to eat," I said. "We need to get to the next job. We are installing a boiler, and we cannot be late."

We continued chatting. I stared down at the pavement while we walked. When we reached about halfway across the lot, a gentleman emerged from behind a nearby vehicle. He was large – about six feet tall and a few hundred pounds. He had thinning, brown hair, and a receding hairline that was shaped like a "v." I assumed he was some sort of businessman considering he was wearing a dress shirt, tie, slacks, and freshly polished black shoes.

He quickly walked towards us, which freaked me out.

"Hey!" he exclaimed, staring at us excitedly.

He pointed to the sign on our van.

"Do you work for them?" he asked.

"Yes," I replied.

"What do you do?" he asked, standing directly in front of us.

We stopped walking.

"I am a plumber," I said slowly, a bit concerned about his intentions.

"It is so wonderful to see a female plumber in the trades!" he exclaimed, outstretching his long, thick arms and embracing me in a smothering hug.

"I am so happy to see you do this!" he yelled.

My face was buried in his armpit.

"Is this seriously happening to me right now?" I thought, inhaling the smell of cologne and armpit. "How the hell do I get out of this now?"

I did not know what to do. My apprentice was standing next to me, and I had a knife in my pocket, so I was not scared, just extremely uncomfortable. The guy stood there, his arms wrapped around me, for what seemed like hours. I felt trapped. He was hugging me so tightly I could not talk. My heart pumped faster.

Finally, my apprentice grabbed the guy's wrist.

"Excuse me, sir," he said. "We are in a hurry."

He pulled open the guy's arms and yanked me back. I gasped for air.

"Oh yeah, yeah," said the guy, as if he did nothing wrong. "You need to get to those emergencies."

He winked. We raced past him. Once we were inside the restaurant, we started laughing. I was freaked out at first, but I was not hurt. The whole incident was so random and unexpected.

"Can you believe that happened?" said my apprentice.

"I thought that guy was going to crush me," I said. "Although I am invincible!" I shouted.

We laughed and laughed. Who would hug a random stranger walking through a parking lot? I wondered if he used that strategy to pick up women. There most likely was something wrong with the guy. It was the only logical explanation.

When we arrived back at our van, thankfully, the guy was gone. We talked about the hug for the rest of the afternoon. It was just something I would never have expected to happen while walking across a parking lot. As a female in the trades, I am accustomed to guys staring at me. In the beginning of my career, it made me uncomfortable, however, after a while it happened so often, I grew accustomed to it.

One time, I was fixing the plumbing in a commercial building. In one hand, I held a two and a half inch, round piece of copper pipe. It stood vertically, reaching up to my shoulder. In the other hand, I had a strip of sand cloth to clean the end of it. While moving the cloth up and down the pipe, I looked up to find three guys staring at me. Their jaws dropped down to the ground. Thinking through the situation, I quickly realized my hand motion along the pipe closely resembled a hand job. Slowly, I lowered the pipe to the ground and smiled. The guys bolted. I think they were more embarrassed than me.

One day, when my apprentice and I walked into a wholesale store to buy some tools, all the men inside looked up and stared as if I were an exotic animal.

"Doesn't that bother you?" asked my apprentice.

"Does what bother me?" I replied.

"That everyone is staring at you," he said, nodding towards the gaping men.

I laughed.

"It used to bother me, but then I figured out why they were staring, so it does not bother me anymore," I said.

"Why is that?" he asked.

"Because I am huge!" I exclaimed, flexing my bicep muscle.

When men stare at me, I have fun with it. When men hug me, it is a different story. I will never get used to it.

NOT SO FANTASTIC
MR. SQUIRREL

Many years ago, I was assigned a job with two other plumbers to install the plumbing in a restaurant. The building was being renovated. For weeks, we worked side-by-side with twenty carpenters and electricians. We installed new appliances in the kitchen and refurnished the bathroom. My two plumber colleagues were big guys. One guy was tall and round. The top of my head aligned with his armpit. The other was a strong man, a literal strongman. He competed in strongman competitions. Every muscle on his body bulged.

From the front door of the restaurant, you could see the seating area in the front and a short hallway in the back, which led to the kitchen. The washrooms were off to the side. The building had an addition to enlarge the kitchen. A small crawl space was dug out underneath. For most of the day, I was working in the washrooms until about 4 p.m. in the afternoon when the strongman approached me.

"I need you to stop what you are doing," he said. "I am working on the kitchen piping. I need to connect the new pipes to the old pipes, but the old pipes are in the crawl space, and I cannot fit under there. Pete cannot fit either."

Pete was the round plumber. It was true. There was no way Pete or the strongman could fit in that tiny crawl space. Being the smallest one on the crew, I often get asked to contort my body into small spaces. I do not mind it. The guys do the heavy lifting, so it is an even trade in my book.

"Okay," I said. "I will do it. Someone has to go under there and glue the connections together, right?"

The strongman smiled.

"Thank you," he said. "C'mon. I will walk you over there."

We walked outside around the back of the building. A piece of worn, gray, plywood covered the opening to the crawlspace. It looked like it had not been touched in years. The strongman pulled it off, revealing a small, square-shaped black hole. I was pretty certain building code laws required a space like that to be bigger.

"Oh, great," I thought. "I cannot get claustrophobic, and if I need to get out, I will need to shimmy backward. There was no way I could turn around."

I shined my flashlight into the hole. It was so dark; I could not see the end of the space. The strongman did not even know if we could reach the connection since he could not crawl in and look himself. That hole of darkness was truly a mystery.

"I am going in!" I announced loudly.

The strongman stood outside the hole to make sure I was safe. Company policy required him to stay there. Channeling my best army crawl, I shimmied my body into the hole. Spider webs smacked my face. Dirt and rocks jabbed into my arms and shins. Beetles and ants scurried along the ground. I could have sworn something was crawling on me; I had that uncomfortable feeling. Fortunately, in Canada, there are not many creepy, crawly bugs that can bite and kill you. So, I knew I was not going to die. I took a deep breath.

"Focus on the job," I muttered to myself. "Find the pipes."

"Are you okay?" yelled the strongman.

"I am fine!" I replied. "Just a lot of bugs in here!"

"Can you see the pipes?" he asked.

I froze, unable to speak. At the end of the crawl space, not too far from my face, a large squirrel was staring at me. I did not see him when I first entered because he blended in with the dirt. His fur was a sandy-brown color. Because my body blocked the entire entrance of the crawl space, he was trapped.

A loud, unrecognizable hissing sound came from his mouth. His body arched like a cat. His tail bushed up, curving over his body. He made sure to show his teeth. The front ones were bigger than the rest. They were not pointed; however, they were sharp enough to mangle my face. His claws dug into the ground like he was about to launch at me. If I did not get out of there quickly, he would scratch my face, or worse, rip out my eye. Considering I was laying on my stomach, and could barely move my arms, I had no way to defend myself. It would look a stereotypical girl fight with me, batting my hands against his razor-sharp claws. I was scared, not like I was confronting-a-cougar or going-to-die scared, but scared, nonetheless. I imagined all the diseases I could catch if he bit me.

I shimmied my body backwards as quickly as possible. I prayed the squirrel would not pounce. I even talked to him.

"It is okay, Mr. Squirrel," I whispered. "This is your space. You win. I get it."

Dirt clouded around me as I pushed my body against the ground. After what seemed like an hour, I was free.

"Are you okay?" asked the strongman.

The blood drained from my face. My hands trembled. I could not find my breath. Jumping slightly to the side of the crawl space entrance, I did the heebie-jeebies dance to shake off the anxiety. Only one word came out of my mouth.

"Squirrel!" I yelled.

Pete came over to find out was happening.

"Squirrel! Squirrel!" I yelled again, pointing frantically to the crawl space.

Crouching down, the strongman shined his flashlight into the darkness.

"He looks as scared as you do!" he exclaimed, laughing.

"Whatever!" I said. "He does not want to be trapped in there!"

The strongman and Pete started cracking up. The more they laughed, the more I relaxed. I began laughing with them. We laughed so loudly; a crowd gathered around us. Everyone wanted a glimpse of the squirrel.

I had to go back in there to finish the job; however I did not want to hurt the squirrel. We chose the path of least resistance – food. We each took a part of our lunch – half a ham sandwich, almonds, and an apple – and placed it in the opening of the crawl space.

"Hopefully, he is hungry," said the strongman.

We walked away to finish other parts of the project. An hour later, we went back to the crawl space. The food was untouched. The squirrel cowered in the corner. Stepping up our game, we found a long piece of pipe, stuck it inside and whipped it around. We hoped it would scare him, not hurt him. Eight tradesmen stood around us to watch the show.

"You guys need to leave," I said. "It is too much commotion for him."

They walked away, bowing their heads in disappointment.

Finally, after twenty minutes, the squirrel darted out, racing across the yard and up a tree.

"Look at him go!" shouted Pete.

"Bye, Mr. Squirrel!" I chimed in. "Thank you for not scratching off my face!"

I successfully shimmied back into the crawl space, found the pipes, and finished the job. The squirrel became a running joke among my coworkers. From that day forward, if they did not want to go into a room to do a job, they would yell, "Squirrel!"

I am lucky it was not a skunk.

THE RED EYE

A couple months ago, my boss received a call from a guy who needed a toilet replaced. It was a brutally cold winter day in Edmonton. Snow piled high. The freezing wind ripped through trees, howling as it moved. No one wanted to go outside, except for people like me who worked around the clock no matter the weather conditions. My boss assigned me the toilet job.

"Bundle up," he said as I was leaving the office. "It is chilly out there."

I slipped on my steel toe boots, which were not made for the winter. We were required to wear steel toe boots for safety reasons. They were so darn expensive, I could only buy one pair, and they were not warm. I bundled up on top though – wearing three pairs of pants, two coats, a hat, scarf, and heavy gloves.

The guy lived on an acre of land, which that day was blanketed in snow. My white van slipped and skidded as I pulled up along the street. It also was not made for the winter. I grabbed my bag of tools and carefully walked up the driveway. The wind whipped against my face. The snow was up to my shins.

The house was a vinyl-sided, yellow bungalow. The front had a large, wooden deck, which was covered in snow. I walked up a set of stairs to reach the front door. The guy opened the door to greet me.

"Hello," I said. "I am Carissa, the plumber. I am here to replace your toilet."

"Uh, yes," he said slowly. "I am Todd. Please come in."

Todd was short, about five-foot-six inches, which is a little taller than me. He had a pale complexion and was extremely skinny. He looked frail like he was sick. His hair was light brown, long and messy. His eyes were slightly red, and his pupils were dilated. He wore ripped, faded jeans and a vintage, rock and roll t-shirt.

"My wife is at work," he said, drawing out every word.

His daughter was in the house too. She looked to be about eighteen years old. She had dirty blond, long hair and wore glasses. I saw her walk behind him and down a hallway, which I assumed led to her room.

I stood in the entry hall as Todd shut the front door. A one-hundred-eighty-pound dog sat in a kennel on my left. He looked like a mix of a Grand Mastiff and Pitbull. He barked loudly.

"Be quiet, Sailor!" yelled Todd.

I followed him down the hall, past the living room, and into the kitchen. A new toilet, which was still in the box, stood next to the counter. The kitchen looked old. It had plain wooden cabinets and a brown, multi-shaded linoleum floor.

"The bathroom is this way," he said.

It seemed like he was having trouble wrapping his mouth around words. He had flimsy pronunciation and spoke abnormally slow.

We walked down another hallway, past his daughter's room and into the bathroom, which was tiny. An old yellow bathtub sat against the back wall. The sink had a ring of rust around its bottom. A small, beat-up, white wooden cabinet sat under the sink. The toilet was leaking. After every flush, sewage water seeped out, pooling onto the brown, linoleum floor. It must had been leaking for a long time. Black mold was starting to grow around the base. The whole room smelled like a mix of sewage, mold and musty, wet wood.

"Let me know if you need anything," said Todd. "I will be in the living room."

I heard him and his daughter chatting, although I could not make out what they were saying. I heard a door open and close. She had left.

I turned off the water. It was obvious whoever installed the toilet did a shoddy job. They screwed it directly into the floor, which with the way the bathroom was designed, was not the right way to do it. The screws were rusted, making it difficult to remove them. First, I used my wrench, and then a saw to cut off the tops. Ten minutes into the job, Todd showed up in the doorway.

"Do you want a beer?" he asked, taking a swig of beer from a bottle in his hand.

It was 10 a.m.

"Uh, no thank you," I said, halfway smiling. "I do not drink, and I am not allowed to drink on the job anyway. I still have to drive, you know."

I wanted to be polite even though I thought it was an odd question, especially before lunch. I guess it was 5 p.m. somewhere, right?

"Okay," he mumbled and went back into the living room.

I finished sawing off the tops of the screws and lifted the toilet off the floor. Twenty minutes later, as I was about to cut the old pipe so I could install a new toilet flange, Todd returned.

"Do you want to smoke a joint?" he asked.

"Uh, no thank you," I replied, laughing nervously. "I cannot do that either. I think I would get fired if I did."

I was astonished and slightly amused that a customer was offering me beer and weed, all before lunch.

"I understand," he said.

Two steps outside the doorway, he swiveled his head back towards me.

"Are you sure?" he asked.

"Yes, I am sure," I said, smiling. "Thank you, though."

I had to maintain my professional, polite demeanor, despite my inner voice screaming, "He is nuts!"

"Do you mind if I smoke one?" he asked.

"Go ahead," I said. "It is your house, after all."

He walked back into the living room and lit up a joint. Considering the bathroom was only a few steps away, I felt like I was getting a second-hand high. A haze creeped down the hallway.

I picked up the old toilet and carried it out the front door. Walking down snow-covered stairs while carrying a sixty-pound, porcelain toilet was no easy feat. I trekked cautiously through the snow, praying I would not slip and fall. Once I reached my van, I placed the toilet in the back and returned to the house. The living room was a giant haze. I could barely see Todd sitting on the couch.

I went back into the bathroom and installed the new toilet.

"I am done!" I yelled. "Do you want to come look?"

He slowly stumbled into the bathroom. His eyes were beet red. His back hunched over. It looked like he was struggling to stand up on his own.

"It looooooks grrrrrreeeat," he said, slurring his words.

I packed up my tools. Todd walked me to the front door. It was almost noon.

"Do you want to do a line before you go?" he asked.

"Is he kidding?" I thought.

I do not use drugs, and it was not even lunchtime yet. He seemed harmless, though. Besides the fact that he was stoned out of his mind, he was also a small person. Not to mention, I had a knife in my pocket and a hammer in my hand.

"Uh, no thank you," I said again.

"What in the world made him think, after offering me beer and weed, which I turned down, that I would want to do a line?" I thought.

"Okay. I understand," he said.

I opened the door and left. On my way back to the office, I called my boss.

"So," he said. "How did the job go? Did you get there alright?"

"Well, yes," I said. "I got here just fine. And the job went well too. Although I did get offered beer, weed and a line of cocaine all before noon."

"Seriously?" asked my boss. I could hear the shock in his voice.

"Yes," I said, laughing.

"You could have called me if you did not feel safe," he said.

"Oh, I felt safe," I said. "He was harmless. In fact, I found the whole thing amusing."

We both laughed.

Usually, on jobs, customers offer me food. Todd was the first and last one who offered me drugs.

SLIP TEASE

First year apprentices are always assigned the crappiest jobs. Those jobs taught me; however, some important life lessons, such as that luxury residential buildings usually have penthouses, and those penthouses may have elevators that open inside the unit.

On a snowy spring day (It is Canada. Are you surprised?), my boss joined me on a job at a luxury condominium building. The building manager hired us to fix a circulation pump for the boiler and haul out a bunch of junk from the mechanical room. The building was gorgeous, one of the most expensive ones in Edmonton. The exterior looked Victorian with large, cream-colored bricks, big windows and terracotta tile on the roof. It had multiple layers of security, including a gate surrounding the exterior of the building, a doorman and a key fob for all residents. Without the fob, they could not use the elevator.

When my boss and I arrived, a waterfall at the entranceway greeted us. The water spilled over chic metallic tiles.

The building manager was waiting for us, with a key fob in-hand.

"The mechanical room is on the roof," he explained. "We have hot water tanks, old pumps, paint cans, boilers and a pile of other junk in there. Please haul out all of it, and fix the pump, of course."

"No problem," replied my boss.

The mechanical room was small and square-shaped. It sat in the middle of the roof, which was covered in snow. The room was packed with junk. We expected the job to take the entire day.

If this were any other job, I would have thought, "Oh great, another crappy job where I just lug stuff back and forth." The building, however, made up for it. The views from the roof were incredible. I could see all of Edmonton and beyond. The snowy landscape stretched for miles.

My boss and I brought a couple tanks and pumps down to our truck.

"I am going to make a phone call," he said before we headed back up. "Can you go up and bring more down?"

"Sure," I replied.

He handed me the key fob.

I went back inside, into the elevator and held the fob against the pad. When the doors opened, I expected to see the snowy roof. To my surprise, I was wrong.

A man was sitting on a couch watching television. The elevator had taken me to his penthouse.

"Uh, hi?" he said.

Until that moment, I had no idea the building had a penthouse, and I had never seen an elevator open directly into an apartment. The fob was only supposed to give me access to the roof; however, the elevator, which was clearly broken, took me straight into this guy's penthouse. The moment was awkward to say the least, especially considering he and his home were gorgeous.

"Um, uh, uh," I stammered.

"Pull it together, Carissa!" screamed my inner voice.

The guy had light brown hair, which was brushed to the side, a muscular build, and turquoise-framed glasses. He wore gray pajama pants and a white t-shirt. He seemed as surprised to see me as I was to see him.

"Can I help you?" he asked.

"I am so sorry," I said.

The elevator doors started closing. I braced my arms between them, refusing to leave on such an awkward note.

"So, which one of my friends sent you?" he asked.

And then things became more awkward. I stood in the elevator, frozen, not understanding the question.

"Excuse me?" I asked nervously.

"Which one of my friends sent you?" he repeated, slowly standing up and walking over to me.

"Uh, no, sir," I said. "My company sent me. I am in the wrong place. Sorry, I should not be here."

"Are my friends coming too?" he asked while standing directly in front of me. "It is weird to have a stripper when you are alone."

I burst out laughing.

"Sir," I said, trying to catch my breath from laughing so hard. "This is not my sexy plumber outfit. This is my actual plumber outfit."

I was wearing baggy, brown coveralls with a t-shirt and sweater underneath, and a baggy, navy-blue zip-up sweater on top. Nothing about my outfit screamed "sexy," nor "stripper." The sweater even had my company's logo sewn onto it.

Notably confused, the guy half-laughed.

"You see, sir," I explained. "I am the plumber. Your building manager hired me to fix a pump in the mechanical room and haul out a bunch of junk."

The guy's laugh grew louder.

"I am sorry!" he exclaimed. "I am getting married this weekend, so I thought this was a pop-up bachelor party or something."

We both laughed uncontrollably.

"Have you been to this building before?" he asked.

"Yes, a couple times," I replied. "I am surprised the fob allowed me to come up to your unit. Is that typical?"

"No," he said. "That is not supposed to happen. I will need to get the building to fix it."

"Well, your place is beautiful," I said.

He flashed a perfectly white-toothed smile.

"Do you want a tour?" he asked.

I knew my boss would be looking for me; however, I was not about to pass up a tour of a gorgeous penthouse unit by a gorgeous penthouse owner.

The place was stunning. The living room had high ceilings with long, wooden beams and walls made of glass. A balcony protruded from every side. Each one had its own, red brick fireplace. A large, four-sided fireplace sat in the middle. The kitchen was covered in dark granite. Pots and pans hung from the ceiling over the island. The master bedroom had light, gray carpeting that was softer than my bed. The master bathroom had steam showers and a bidet. He turned the second bedroom into an office. Built-in bookshelves filled with books lined each wall. The place was covered in art. Except for a portrait of a pug dog, the art was abstract.

The tour took ten minutes, which was enough time for me to "ooh" and "aww" over everything. Surprisingly, however, that incident was not the most interesting part of my day.

I returned to the snowy roof and walked into the mechanical room. My boss was piling junk to carry down. He seemed to not realize I disappeared for ten minutes.

"Let's haul out this tank and these pipes," he said.

We carried the stuff to our truck and went back up to the roof. The views were breathtaking. Wanting to soak it all in for a few minutes, I took a slight detour, walking closer to the edge of the roof, while my boss made a beeline to the mechanical room. We talked as we walked, or more like yelled so we could hear each other.

"What should we get next?" he yelled.

"I don't know. Maybe some of the paint cans?" I responded.

"What about the last boiler?" he asked.

Woosh! Suddenly, I started falling. It felt like the edge of the roof crumbled beneath my feet, leaving me free-falling into oblivion. My stomach jumped into my throat. I did not understand how I fell or what was happening. One second the ground was under my feet; the next second it was gone. I was terrified.

"This is it," I thought. "I am going to die right now."

Thud! My back hit the ground. Darkness surrounded me, except for a hole into the sky far above my eyes. The fall knocked the wind out of me. I could not breathe. Gasping for air, I got my wits about me.

"Where am I?" I thought.

Silence and darkness crept around me. I wiggled my toes, rolled my ankles, and stretched my arms. Nothing felt broken. Slowly, I stood up.

"Help!" I shouted. "Help me! Please, I need help, please!"

A slight echo bounced around me. The chilly air smelled musty, like rotting wood. Everything was so dark; I could not make out any objects. It looked like I was standing in a black hole. Blinking repeatedly, I tried seeing through the darkness. It did not look like something was going to attack me, which made me relax slightly.

"Holy crap!" I heard my boss yell.

"Hey!" I yelled back, feeling relieved.

His face appeared in the hole.

"What the hell happened to you?" he asked.

"I fell," I said. "I was walking along the roof, closer to the edge when suddenly I dropped."

"I had no idea what happened!" he exclaimed. "You did not respond to my question, and then you just disappeared! I thought you visited someone for dinner!"

I laughed. He thought I fell through the building into someone's kitchen, which coincidentally, would have been the handsome man's kitchen I was standing in an hour ago. He lived directly below the rooftop.

"Are you okay?" asked my boss.

"Yes, I am fine. I did not land on my head. My limbs are intact. Nothing is bleeding," I said. "I am in this weird hole. I would like to get out."

"Okay," he yelled. "I will be back in a few minutes."

Apparently, my boss ran through the halls of the building, screaming for someone to call 9-1-1. A group of tenants congregated along with the building manager. They all came to my rescue. My boss had a harness and rope in-hand. The building manager brought extra plywood to place over the rotted wood where I fell.

"It is okay!" he shouted. "You are in a swimming pool!"

"I am in a what?" I replied.

"Yes," he said. "When they built this building, the developer installed a swimming pool on the roof. He did not consider, however, the weight of the water, which would have been too heavy for this roof. So, he left it empty and covered it with plywood. You probably fell about eight feet."

It would have been nice to know about the pool before we started working on the roof. The snow blanketed the rotting plywood, making it blend in with everything else.

My boss threw down the harness. I slipped it on and hooked it to the rope. While I could not see what everyone was doing at the top, I heard it loud and clear.

"Pull!" yelled the building manager.

"Are you okay?" shouted my boss.

My body dangled in the darkness.

"Yes! I am fine!" I replied.

"One, two, three, pull!" yelled the building manager.

"Are you sure you are okay?" asked my boss again.

"Yes! Just keep going please!" I insisted.

"Ehhhhh!" grunted a few people, rather dramatically.

It could not have been that much of a struggle. I only weighed one-hundred-twenty pounds.

When my body reached the top, I clutched the ground and crawled over the edge.

"Woohoo! We did it!" cheered the building manager and my boss. The tenants started clapping.

I smiled, relieved to be out of there, unscathed.

The rest of the day was uneventful. My boss kept asking if I was okay. I appreciated his concern. We went back the next day to finish the job. In the pile of junk, I found leftover Halloween decorations, which included a glow in the dark skeleton that was the same size as me. I taped it to my clothes, hid in a corner, and jumped out to scare my boss. I figured I could get away with stuff like that while he was still so happy that I was alive.

A MOMENT OF REFLECTION

The best part about plumbing is that I am always learning something new. Every day is a new adventure with different problems to solve and people to meet. Admittedly, when I chose to be a plumber, I did not factor in the customer service part of it. Interacting with people from different countries and cultures is a key part of my job. Since I started my career, I have significantly improved my language skills. Not only can I understand a variety of accents, but I can also understand different languages. Plumbing is a universal career. Everybody needs it, some places more than others.

I have also learned a lot from listening to customers, although they sometimes overshare. For some reason, some people think of me as a therapist. They talk about their terrible boyfriends and broken hearts. I usually just listen and continue working. My cardinal rule is to never offer advice.

Elderly customers share the best stories. Many of them are widows, yet their stories are uplifting. One woman told me a story about her late husband, who was a war hero. I could have stayed there all day listening to her.

One of my most interesting jobs was at the army base in Edmonton. I was hired to install hose bibs on some housing units. While working, I talked to soldiers about the different kinds of weapons they used and the conflicts in Iraq and Afghanistan. It was interesting to hear their point of view.

I really enjoy plumbing. Some people wrinkle their nose at me because they think it is a gross career; however there is so much more to it than unclogging toilets. Plumbing is problem-solving. It is figuring out what is not working and why it is broken. In Canada, many plumbers flunk out of school during their first or second year because the course load is too rigorous. It is a tough trade that requires analytical thinking and patience.

The trade is becoming more progressive. People are not as surprised anymore when a woman shows up at their doorstep. Occasionally, a man who unsuccessfully tried to fix a drain or pipe watches me fix it in fifteen minutes and gets slightly huffy. He tries to hide it, although I can tell he is bothered by my existence. During my first week working as a plumber, the guy who was training me asked me to flush a toilet and urinal.

"Did they flush properly?" he asked.

"The toilet did," I replied.

"What about the urinal?" he asked.

"I think it did, but I have never flushed a urinal before," I replied.

He burst out laughing. I was the first woman he ever trained. It did not occur to him that I had never used a urinal.

I do not plan to leave the plumbing business any time soon. Plumbers tend to get back problems and hernias, so eventually, many years down the road, I hope to focus on managing a company instead of working on tools. I recently started my own company, and it has taken off quickly. I hope to soon hire my first employee, keep growing the business and then one day run the business from an office. Of course, I would go on occasional service calls. I would miss the tools too much if I ducked out completely.

CHAPTER 3
TODD

When I was twenty-seven years old, an aneurysm exploded in my brain. Most people die on the spot when something like that happens, however not me. I spent eighteen hours on the operating table and was back to normal shortly afterward, although maybe a bit goofier. I did not even need physical therapy.

Once I was back on my feet, I needed to find a job. I had always been good with tools, so when I saw an advertisement for a plumber opening, I applied. The owner hired me as an apprentice. Eventually, I got my plumbing license. Then, unexpectedly, after twenty-one years of working as a full-time plumber for that same owner, he fired me. He wanted me to rip off an elderly lady, which I refused to do, so he told me to leave, forever.

Losing my job was not the end of the world. I remained in close contact with many clients who respected and trusted me. I owned a van and had a license. So, for the past twenty years, I have been working on my own. Last year, I tried to retire. I even sold my van. A guy called me, however, offering three thousand dollars for a job. How could I say no? To me, shit smells like money.

My only self-struggle after all these years working as a plumber is that most of my work you cannot see. I have created complex, beautiful copper puzzles, and then a wall goes up and covers all of it. After working tirelessly on a job, solving problems no one else could solve, it is a bit frustrating no one can see my feat.

I pride myself on being a "no callback" plumber. When I come to your house to fix a leaking toilet, it is fixed permanently. I do not get calls a week later saying the toilet is leaking again. I am good at what I do.

I also have a strong stomach. During my more than forty years of plumbing, I have only dry heaved once. A lady asked me to unclog her sink. I removed the cleanout plug and saw it was jammed with SpaghettiOs. When I stuck my finger in them, they exploded on my shirt. Those SpaghettiOs must have been in there for two years, at least. They smelled worse than shit. I dry heaved a few times. After finishing the job, I ripped off my clothes and drove home in my underwear.

Except for that day, whenever I go into people's homes, no matter how horrible they smell, I sniff and say, "Ah, it smells like money."

I am Todd, and these are my diaries.

THE UNWANTED TEASE

My customers are all repeats. I have never advertised a day in my life. Oftentimes on jobs, I hire other plumbers to work with me. Sometimes they receive a bit more than they ask for, and I am not talking about money.

About a year ago, a woman called me about a clogged sewer and busted pipe in her 91-year-old mother's home. I knew the daughter well. She had hired me to fix pretty much all her plumbing problems. Whenever she called, she opened the conversation in a strange, unconventional way. That day was no exception.

"I want to go on your boat," she said, before saying "hello."

I own three boats. Whenever the daughter sees me, she asks to go on one of them. I have never had her aboard.

"What is the problem?" I asked, steering the conversation back to the job.

"My mom's sewer is clogged, and there is a leak," she explained.

"I'll be right over," I said.

I asked another plumber to come with me.

"Mike, whatever you do," I explained on our way to the house. "Do not talk to the mother."

I learned that lesson the hard way. I talked to the mother during the previous job I worked on at her house. She talked my ear off for four hours.

We pulled up to the house, which was a brick, ranch-style home with white trim around the windows. The daughter answered the door.

"I want to go on your boat," she said again.

"Can you show us the problems?" I asked, ignoring her comment.

She walked us downstairs into the basement. Boxes were scattered everywhere. The room smelled like shit, or shall I say...money. We weaved through the boxes to get to the clogged sewer and broken pipe. Water came up from the floor drain, which needed to be rodded. Considering it was later in the day, we decided to leave and come back in the morning. On our way out, we saw the mother. She was wearing striped, blue and white pants. The waist was up to her chest.

"Hello," said Mike stupidly.

Because of that quick, "hello," we were stuck there for two hours. Finally, when I saw a window to politely escape, I gave the daughter my price and told her we would return the next day.

"Mike, do not talk to the mother!" I reminded him on our way to the house the next day. "As you saw, we will be there forever if you do!"

The daughter answered the door again.

"I want to go on your boat!" she exclaimed, holding the door open.

"Hello, again," I said, walking past her towards the basement door.

Once again, we weaved through the boxes and stopped at the sewer. It was clogged with tree roots. We rodded them out and replaced the copper pipe. The whole job took a couple hours.

We went back upstairs. The mother was sitting at the kitchen table with her checkbook in front of her.

"We are done," I said, quickly and curtly.

I stood there watching her, praying she would write the check in silence so we could leave.

"How are you today?" asked Mike, like I never even warned him.

I subtly shot him a dirty look. Without skipping a beat, the mother launched into a monologue, talking and talking. Two and a half hours later, just as I was about to lose my cool, she said:

"When I was in high school, they called me 'little titties.' Do you want to see them?"

My mouth dropped open. Never had I imagined a 91-year-old woman volunteering to show me her tits. I fidgeted awkwardly. Not one bone in my body wanted to see her tits. I also knew if I said anything else, we would see her tits and end up staying there for another four hours. Mike stood there silently, for once. His face blanched. His eyes looked like a deer in headlights.

"I want to go on your boat," said the daughter, breaking the silence.

"Yeah, you can go on the boat whenever you want," I said, grabbing the check from the mother's hand and running out of there.

Once inside our truck, I verbally reprimanded Mike.

"I told you not to talk to her," I said loudly. "Why, why, why did you talk to her?"

He did not say anything. We sat there silently the entire drive home. He knew he messed up, and I could see by his wide-eyed stare, he regretted it.

THE ASSHOLE, THE BITCH AND THE FUNGUS-PHOBE

During the early days of my plumbing career, I would work five, six, sometimes seven jobs a day and all hours of the night. I met many kinds of people, most of whom loved me. Some felt otherwise; however, I did not mind. You cannot win over everyone.

One time a woman called me about a clogged sewer in her home. It was 8 p.m.

"Can you come tonight?" she asked. "I need this sewer unclogged."

"Okay," I said. "I will be right over."

I pulled up to the house. Since it was dark outside, I do not remember what it looked like. When the woman answered the door, I immediately told her how much the job would cost. I always prefer to be upfront about money so that I do not have to chase it down later.

"Go ahead and do it," she said. "The cleanout is in the back."

Since the cleanout was outside, I did not have to go inside the house. I walked over to it and started rodding. Ten minutes into the job, I felt the rodder hit the blockage. When I pulled it out, about two hundred baby wipes came with it, wrapped around the end of the rodder.

Baby wipes do not disintegrate, which is why no one should be flushing them down the toilet.

"You should not throw baby wipes in the toilet," I told the woman.

Her head poked out the back door of the house.

"I do not have kids," she said.

"Huh?" I said, puzzled.

"My husband has an asshole problem," she stated matter-of-factly like it was no big deal.

"Okay, that is too much information for me," I said.

I wrote her a ticket and left.

Everyone thinks plumbers are psychiatrists. I do not give a crap about her husband's asshole problems. I went to her house to do a job, and that was it. If additional information, like asshole problems, has nothing to do with me, I do not want to know about it.

Switching gears for a moment, I have one cardinal rule for every job I do – my shoes stay on.

People always say, "Do not look at my house! I have not cleaned it in weeks," which is precisely why I refuse to take off my shoes in anyone's house. I do not want a toe fungus.

A long time ago, one woman expected me to break my rule. She called because her basement flooded. When I pulled up in my van, she ran out of the house, her arms flailing wildly in the air.

"Do not park in the driveway!" she yelled.

"Okay," I said, not wanting to cause trouble, although I did not appreciate her yelling at me first thing in the morning.

I parked the van in the street. Knowing her basement was flooded with what I could only imagine was not a pleasant substance, I wanted to glue my shoes to my feet.

She stood in the doorway as I approached the house. She was a shorter woman, with short brown hair and beady eyes.

"Take off your shoes," she demanded.

"What?" I asked, thinking she must be crazy.

"Take off your shoes," she repeated with a nasty bite in her voice.

"Take off your shirt," I replied.

"Get out of here!" she yelled, throwing me out of the house.

Losing that job did not bother me for a second. I was not about to walk around in socks in her feces-filled, watered-down basement. Besides, I had plenty of clients.

People love me. I have customers whose kids were babies when I first started doing jobs for them. Now, the kids are graduating college, and I am still doing jobs for them. I have older people who call me, and if they remind me of my grandmother, I do not charge them.

The assholes are the ones I do not need in my life.

One time a lady called me about a clogged bathtub. I went to her house, which was a ranch-style, red brick home with white trim around the windows. She greeted me at the door and walked me back to the bathroom.

The tub had a couple inches of water in it. The rest of the room was dry.

I assessed the tub and gave her a price.

"That is fine," she said. "Can you just fix it?"

"Sure," I said. "I can do it now."

I was carrying a tool that cleared the tub easily. I did not even have to rod it. When I finished, I double-checked to make sure the water was draining properly.

"I am done," I told the woman. "I left the invoices in my van so I will need to go get them."

The woman looked inside the tub.

"You are not done," she said.

"What do you mean?" I asked. "The bathtub runs perfectly."

"You have to clean it," she said as if cleaning was built into my services.

"I am not a maid," I said, trying to subdue my anger. "I am not cleaning your tub. You asked me to clear it, not clean it."

She paid me the money, and I left.

That was the last time I saw her, thankfully.

WHEN YOU GOTTA GO...

I can never stay at a house all day. It makes me nervous. My jobs are usually two hours at most. Then I head to the next one. If a job is going to take longer, I outsource it to other plumbers in the area. Every morning and night, I make sure to check in with the client. That way, the client knows I am overseeing the project while the other crews do the work.

That was the arrangement for one project in Highland Park, Illinois. An older lady owned twelve townhomes. They were made of brick with black trim around the rectangular windows. Each one had two floors. They looked new. The lady was looking for a plumber to install drain tile in the garages of all the homes. A contractor recommended me for the job. I hired another plumbing crew to assist. We went to her house in the morning, so I could introduce myself as the project lead. The lady answered the door with a smile.

"Hello," she said. "You must be Todd."

"I am, ma'am," I replied. "It is nice to meet you."

After walking her through the steps of the project, I left to spend the day on my boat. The crew continued working on the garages. They dug out perimeters to install the tile. The job took all day, even with eight guys dedicated to it.

I returned to the lady's house around 5 p.m. that afternoon.

"Hello again," she said with a smile.

"Hello," I replied. "I will need a check."

"Why don't you come in?" she asked, opening the door a little wider.

She was such a nice lady. I did not want to come off as a money-grubbing rude guy, so I accepted her invitation and went inside. The place was clean, modern, and nice.

"Can you write out the check please?" I asked, standing in the entryway.

"Give me minute," she said. "I need to go get my checkbook."

She practically crawled up a staircase which must have led to her bedroom or an office. I had never seen a person move so slowly. To make matters worse, I desperately had to pee.

Another one of my cardinal rules is that l will never use the bathroom in a customer's house, no matter how badly I have to go. The reason being is that if I say to a customer - "May I use your bathroom?" – she would assume I am taking a shit. For the record, I would never take a dump in someone's house.

I waited and waited, holding in my pee. My stomach began to cramp. I shifted my weight from side to side, performing the classic "I gotta go" dance.

After a few minutes, and no sign of the lady, I could not take it anymore. I opened the door, walked outside by her pine needle bushes, dropped my pants, and let it flow. Once I finished, besides the pine needles stuck in my ass, I was good to go. I pulled up my pants and headed back inside. The lady finally came back downstairs and handed me the check.

"See you tomorrow," I said.

"Yes! Have a good evening," she replied, still smiling.

The next morning, I headed back to her house.

"Can you please come in?" she said, opening the door slightly wider. "I want to show you something."

I went inside. She walked me to her glass top kitchen table. A photograph was placed in the center of it.

"What is this?" she asked, pointing to the photograph.

"What the heck is she talking about?" I asked myself, looking closer at the photograph.

A light bulb flickered on in my head. The photograph was of me, standing with my pants down, peeing in her bushes.

"My neighbor took this picture," she explained. "She brought it over this morning."

"I had to go to the bathroom, so I went in your bushes," I stated, not embarrassed at all. I do not get embarrassed.

"Why didn't you use my bathroom?" asked the lady.

Surprisingly, she did not seem upset. On the contrary, it looked like she felt guilty that I was so desperate I went in her bushes instead of in her bathroom.

"It is impolite to use your bathroom," I said, appreciating her delicate reaction to the photograph.

"Next time, you should know you can use my bathroom," she said, smiling.

That job took three weeks to complete. I did not pee in her bushes again; however, it was not because I felt ashamed or embarrassed nor because I went in her bathroom instead. I simply did not have to go.

THE LOG THAT CLOGGED

Nothing grosses me out. And believe me, I have seen some disgusting things. One time, a woman called around 10 a.m. about a clogged vanity sink in her bathroom.

"Can you come by today?" she begged. "My bathroom sink is clogged. I really need it unclogged as soon as possible."

"Okay," I said. "I will be over soon."

I pulled up to her ranch-style, vinyl-sided home. When she opened the door, before even introducing myself, I gave her my price.

"No problem," she said. "I can pay that. Just please fix it."

She was an older woman. Her hair was starting to gray. She wore sweatpants and slippers, which clicked as she walked me down the hallway into the bathroom. The vanity sink was made of white porcelain. A light gray, wooden cabinet sat underneath it. Water flooded the bowl of the sink, almost to the top.

"I will leave you alone," said the woman. "If you need anything, just holler."

I removed the pop-up stopper at the bottom of the sink's bowl and ran the water. Using an air ram, I then cleared the pipe. After double-checking to make sure the sink was working properly, I looked to my right. Almost touching my hand, a glass jar of used Q-Tips sat on the vanity. There must have been a hundred of them in the jar. I knew they were used because the tips were yellow, with specks of crust on the ends of some of them. She must have cleaned her ears and then immediately placed the Q-Tip in the jar. Despite it being the most disgusting collection of anything I had ever seen, I was not nauseous. I thought it was disgusting and weird, but it did not affect me physically.

I told the woman I finished the job, collected my money, and left. Of course, I did not say anything about the collection of crusty Q-Tips. I have manners!

One time, a guy called me around 7 p.m. He owned a house in Mount Prospect, Illinois, which he rented out to a young couple.

"You gotta come help," he said. "My tenants' sewer is clogged. They cannot flush the toilet. Can you meet me tonight at the house, please?"

"Okay, I am on my way," I said.

The guy sounded desperate, and those were the days when I worked all hours of the night anyway.

It was so dark outside I could barely see the house. Clearly, the guy skimped on exterior lighting. When I pulled into the driveway, he shined a huge flashlight on the front of my van.

"Thanks for coming so late," he said. "Follow me."

We walked around the house into the backyard. Tall, dark trees surrounded us.

"Here is the cleanout," said the guy.

One of the tenants opened the back door. Amidst the darkness, I could only see her silhouette. She stood in the doorway watching me. The guy shined the flashlight on the cleanout, so I could see what I was doing. I unscrewed the cap. The cleanout was filled with water. I used my rodder to unclog it. Once it popped, I investigated the pipe. About seven inches down, I saw an enormous turd. It looked like a nine-pound roast. It must have measured six by ten inches, and it clogged the entire sewer.

"Look at the size of that turd! It looks like it came out of a cow!" I exclaimed while doing a turd dance. "This is the biggest turd I have ever seen!"

Whoever laid that turd, I could not believe the person was still walking. They must have needed stitches to sew up their asshole.

"Shhhh," the homeowner whispered loudly, with his finger positioned vertically over his mouth. "The tenant is standing right there!"

He nudged his head towards the doorway. I knew the tenant was standing there; however, I did not care. That turd was impressive. The wife or husband should be proud of it. If there were a largest human turd trophy, that one would take the cake.

I finished the job and turd danced my way to the van. Usually, too much toilet paper clogs sewers. That night was the first time I had seen a turd clog an entire sewer.

A MOMENT OF REFLECTION

If you cannot go to work and have fun, laugh, and make money, then there is no point in going to work. Plumbing is fun. My colleagues and I have secret code names for certain treasures we find, which are quite comical. We call corn, for example, "gold teeth." You can chew corn for an hour, and it will still come back out like it came straight out of the can. We call tampons "white mice." That one speaks for itself. No matter how wacky clients act, or how disgusting the job may be, we always find a way to have fun, and not take ourselves too seriously.

Even when encounters get weird, I laugh them off. For example, one lady offered me a blow job in exchange for my services.

"Thanks for the offer, ma'am," I said. "But I would rather have the money."

She threw me out of her house.

One time, I was laying on the floor, working under a bathroom sink, when I heard loud, moaning sounds coming from the attached bedroom. The customer was playing with herself, right in front of me. I called it "great action" and laughed it off.

Even when I almost had a severe allergic reaction while on a job, I laughed it off. The woman had twenty-nine cats and a giant kiddie swimming pool full of litter. I am allergic to cats, so I left her house minutes after arriving, and chuckled the whole way home. You typically do not encounter people who own twenty-nine cats.

Another time, a lady called me about a clogged toilet. I went to her house, rodded the toilet and pulled out a nine-inch tampon, which was really a bunch of tampons melded into one.

"It is not mine!" she exclaimed.

"Uh, ma'am," I replied, laughing. "It is your sewer. No one else lives here. This is yours."

During my forty-plus years of plumbing, I have seen and smelled pretty much everything. Nothing surprises or bothers me.

I lost my whole family. I do not have to be anywhere except for right here, in this moment, unclogging a toilet, fixing a pipe, or doing whatever other plumbing job I was hired to do. And I am enjoying every minute of the ride.

CHAPTER 4
DEAN

I rodded my first sewer when I was twelve years old. My uncle owned a plumbing business and would let me join him on service calls.

"Go rod that sewer," he always said, the minute we pulled up to the home.

After I finished the jobs, he used the earnings to buy me pizza. Those years marked the beginning of my 35-year career as a plumber.

Today, I work independently, mainly servicing customers from Chicago to the Wisconsin border. I have worked on homes, commercial buildings, factories, even swimming pools. I love plumbing because it is like playing with a Tinkertoy set every day. Whether it is figuring out the right sized pipes and where they should go, or discovering toilet "treasures," each job brings new adventures.

I am Dean, and these are my diaries.

THE OLD MEN AND THE XXXL

On a wintry November day, I received a call from the manager of a popular fast food restaurant.

"Hi Dean," he said. "The toilet in the men's bathroom is clogged. Can you please come fix it as soon as possible?"

Restaurant jobs tend to be easier than working on homes and less of a headache. When you pull up to a house, you typically encounter one of three types of people – hoarders, "normal" people, or homeowners who are so obsessed with cleanliness that if they see my rodding machine in the house they will freak out (I have had customers pay three thousand dollars just so I did the job while remaining outside). With restaurants, jobs are pretty cut and dry and have the same problems. The women's bathroom is also always dirtier than the men's bathroom.

When I arrived at the restaurant, I approached the ordering counter. A handful of people were eating in the dining area, munching on burgers and fries. The manager came out to greet me.

"Thank you for coming so quickly," he said. "Follow me. The bathroom is over here."

We walked down a short hallway and into the bathroom. He pointed to the clogged toilet.

"There it is," he said. "Let me know if you need anything."

Like most clogged toilets, feces and crumpled toilet paper filled the bowl to the brim. Most people would have found the stench unbearable; however it was business-as-usual for my nose. The smell of crap, no matter how long it has sat in the bowl, does not faze me.

Truthfully, I get more grossed out by the smell of dog crap than human crap.

I began rodding the toilet, trying to catch whatever was clogging it, but nothing was in there. I pulled out the toilet to rod deeper into the line, and still, nothing came out. Two and a half hours later, I stood there puzzled.

"If nothing is catching on the rod, what the heck is clogging the toilet?" I said to myself.

The manager must have sensed my bewilderment, or maybe freaked out when he saw I pulled the toilet and carried in more equipment. He called another plumbing team to assist. Two men walked through the door.

"Hey, I am Billy, and this is Mike. The manager called us. What is going on? This job was supposed to take thirty minutes. The manager says you have been here for a couple hours," said Billy.

"I rodded the toilet. I rodded the line. Whatever is in there will not snag," I explained.

"Let's rod it again," said Mike.

We each took turns rodding. We rodded, rodded, and rodded. Finally, something caught. Like three fishermen pulling a giant bass out of the water, we all grasped the rodder and yanked it upwards. Something that looked like a crumpled, black t-shirt was wrapped around the rodder. It was lathered in poop and toilet paper. When we untangled it, we saw it was not a t-shirt. It was a pair of XXXL boxer shorts.

"Holy smokes!" I exclaimed. "I have never seen a pair of underwear that big!"

All three of us cracked up in disbelief. We showed the manager our new treasure. He was not laughing.

"Holy crap!" he exclaimed. "I need to get my camera. Stay right there."

He wanted to take pictures to send to the corporate office. The job took a few hours, which was much longer than he had expected and more costly. He needed to justify the expense.

Rolling with laughter, Mike and Billy left. I put the toilet back together and cleaned the bathroom. Of course, I threw away the underwear.

When I first started working as a plumber, pulling things out of toilets, like XXXL underwear, was always a "wow, holy crap" moment that stuck with me for days. Now, after encountering so many of them during the years, those "holy crap" moments last about ten minutes.

One time, I received a service call to unclog a toilet in an apartment. Before I could even introduce myself to the renter, he dove into denying that he clogged the toilet. He repeated the denial five or six times. After all, if his landlord found out he was the culprit, the renter would have to pay my service fee out of pocket.

Unfortunately for the renter, the denial became meaningless. I opened the toilet lid, stuck my rod into the sea of poop and toilet paper, and pulled out his driver's license.

"It looks like you are paying for this," I said, handing him the license.

"Aw, crap," he said, defeated.

FIFTEEN SHADES OF RED

While my "holy crap" moments are now minimal, there was one call I will never forget. A woman needed help unclogging her toilet. She allegedly did not know who clogged it, even though she was alone in her own house.

"Hello," I said, knocking on the door.

The woman opened it nonchalantly. She looked to be in her late thirties. She had curly, brown hair, brown eyes, and was wearing a floral-patterned shirt and blue jeans.

"Hello," she said. "Please come in. The bathroom is over here."

She led me through her pristine home. It was clean, comfortable, and full of high-end fixtures. Chandeliers hung from the ceiling in almost every room. The bathroom had a light gray, tiled floor, with a rectangular-shaped, white porcelain sink and vanity, and a steam shower encased in glass. I began laying out my tools. She stood in the doorway, watching my every move.

I lifted the toilet seat. The bowl was filled to the brim with feces and toilet paper. The sight and smell were not a big deal for someone like me who has seen it all. I stuck my rod into the mess. Just three inches down, I felt a blockage. I tried pushing the rod down further; however, it would not budge.

The woman continued standing there, silently watching.

The blockage piqued my curiosity. It was unusual to feel a blockage so close to the brim. Knowing something was not right, I did what any dedicated, experienced, and bewildered plumber would do. I rolled up my sleeve and stuck my hand inside the bowl. Reaching down the hole, I felt something hard. I tried pulling on it but to no avail. I pulled harder. It would not move.

With no alternative option, I removed the toilet and brought it outside. The woman followed me. I rinsed out the bowl with a hose and turned the toilet upside down.

"What the....oh shit!" I exclaimed.

Staring me in the face was a pink, fleshy head – not a human head of course. It was the head of a dildo.

Reaching into the back of the toilet, I pushed it up, then grabbed the head and yanked it out. The thing was longer than a foot, and its flexibility was impressive. Stretching fourteen inches down a toilet bowl is not an easy feat for a large hunk of anything. My guess is the woman had flushed the toilet at least a dozen times and pushed it down manually before the bowl started to clog.

The woman's face turned fifteen shades of red.

"Oh, um, ah," she muttered, unable to say anything else.

"Do you want this, or do you want me to throw it away?" I asked, muscling everything in my power to contain the laughter that was about to burst out of my mouth.

No matter the situation, I always must act like a professional, even when a giant dildo is dangling from my hand.

Humiliated, the woman looked down at the ground. She then briskly walked away.

"I am getting my checkbook," she yelled over her shoulder.

I cleaned up, reinstalled the toilet, collected my check (the woman did not look me in the eye while handing it over) and left. I took the dildo with me. There was no way I was about to throw away that kind of trophy. I ended up tossing it into my cousin's truck, paying forward the surprise.

A year later, the woman's husband called. He needed me to rod a sewer. When I arrived at the house, he did not say a word about the dildo. I am not sure he even knew about it. I never saw his wife again.

A PAUSE ON POOP

On service calls, I meet people from all walks of life. Some of their homes are a complete mess, while others are so stark white, I am afraid to breathe the wrong way when I walk inside. I have found cabinets filled with drugs, and multi-million-dollar homes with lawn furniture inside because the owners cannot afford a couch. I have seen many people scraping by on social security, especially elderly folks, who count every dollar each day, and ration food for the week so they do not go over budget. Despite their troubles, those people are so generous and kind. They take care of their neighbors, which includes their plumbers.

I want to put aside the poop for a moment and discuss the good people I have encountered in this world. I realize it is not as funny, and I hope you continue reading. I have met so many kind-hearted people who go above and beyond to treat others with respect and appreciation. Their stories deserve to be shared.

Any time my uncle and I saw someone in bad shape, we tried to help. We offered to do jobs for free, although most customers insist on paying something to maintain their dignity. So, for a one-hundred-dollar job, we would charge twenty dollars to make the customer feel like he or she was paying for something.

I will never forget one elderly woman. She was a real spitfire. She called because her sewer was clogged with tree roots. When we arrived at her house, she greeted us with a pleasant smile and led us to her kitchen. It looked like it was from the 1950s, and was spotless, unlike my kitchen. She was a typical grandmother-type, wearing a pink robe, sipping her morning coffee, which she drank black. She liked sugar but could only use a small amount each week due to her limited budget and did not want to waste it on coffee.

When we went down into her basement and saw the sewer, I could see she had never had it rodded before. We were there for 4 ½ hours, pulling tree roots from the sewer. They were so thick that by the end, we had filled eight buckets with nothing but roots.

"How much will this cost?" she asked when we were finished.

"It is usually sixty dollars to rod a sewer," I said. "But, please pay us twenty."

We did not want to charge her anything; however she refused to let us do the job for free. She paid us the money, and we left.

We came back regularly for eight years to rod her sewer. On our second visit, she surprised us. When we came up from the basement, she had a whole plate of cookies waiting for us. She used her entire allotment of sugar for the month to make us cookies and continued making them every time we came to help. What a nice lady.

In another situation, a landlord called me. One of his homes had a clogged sewer. He needed us to rod it. The woman who rented the house ran a free daycare for all the kids in the neighborhood. If their parents were working, she would watch their kids for as long as they needed, at no cost.

My uncle and I pulled up to her house. It was a small, ranch-style home with gray vinyl siding and a small porch.

"Are you the plumbers?" she asked when we knocked on the door.

"Yes, ma'am. Nice to meet you," I said.

"Come in!" she said, flashing a big smile.

Kids were running around everywhere. They ranged from two to four-years-old. She handled them as if she were a sergeant and grandmother - no-nonsense, yet plenty of love. We retrieved our equipment from our truck and went downstairs to rod the sewer. The job took about an hour.

"Wait. Here, please take this," she said, as we were about to leave.

She gave us a home-baked sweet potato pie. She made it while we were working, in addition to watching all those kids. I could not believe it. Admittedly, sweet potato pie is not my favorite thing in the world, however her sweet potato pie.... I would kill to have that recipe.

We took care of her house six or seven more times, and every time she sent us home with a sweet potato pie.

Another customer had a six-acre garden. He was an elderly gentleman, eighty-something-years-old, living on ten acres of property. He worked from sun up to sundown tending the garden. Whatever he harvested, he kept a portion of it and donated the rest. Every week he loaded an old, rusty pick-up truck with fifteen to twenty barrels of tomatoes, peppers, cucumbers, and other vegetables, and dropped them off at food pantries in the area. In the fall, he picked apples and delivered them to shelters and churches.

He called us because his septic tank was overflowing. We pumped it, sucking out the water through our truck. The job would typically cost three to four hundred dollars; however my uncle only charged him sixty dollars. The man's house was so run-down. He had chronic problems with the septic system, especially after a heavy rain. Every time we came by to fix it, he insisted on sending us home with several barrels of home-grown vegetables.

One time he told us he tended the entire garden by hand.

"I have to turn the garden up," he said.

"How do you do that?" asked my uncle.

"I use a shovel," he said, matter-of-factly like it was no big deal to turn up a six-acre garden with one shovel.

My uncle had a friend who was a farmer. We asked him to go over to the man's house, fertilize the garden, till it and turn over the soil, at no cost, of course.

Those kinds of people bring so much goodness to the world. I feel honored to have known them.

NAILED IT!

Most plumbers prefer working on new construction projects versus home service calls, which oftentimes require more work than solely fixing a plumbing problem. I cannot count the number of times I have gone into a customer's basement only to find twenty years of accumulated junk which takes me forty-five minutes to move out of the way so I can change out the water heater.

New construction jobs tend to be easier with less drama and crap attached to them (literally and figuratively). We just walk in, do the job we were called to do, and leave. It is cut and dry work, and sometimes a nice break. So, when my cousin and I got a call to install the plumbing in a home under construction, we were looking forward to it.

We arrived at the home at 6 a.m. The carpenters were already there, prepping the walls for drywall. They were a team of four – three seasoned carpenters and one apprentice, who looked to be around eighteen years old. Despite his young age, however, he acted like he knew everything about carpentry.

When we started drilling our holes, I overheard the apprentice get lippy with his superiors.

"You are doing that wrong," he said to one of the older carpenters.

"The plumbers are hacking up all our work," he said to another carpenter, loudly enough to make sure we heard him.

"This is how we should be doing it," he stated to another much more experienced carpenter.

"Shut up and do your job!" roared the head carpenter, finally. "Or you are not going to like what is going to happen."

From the next room, my cousin and I kept working, laughing under our breath. The apprentice spat out demands and insults for two more hours.

"Alright. That is it!" shouted the head carpenter.

We heard a scuffle, then a nail gun shooting repeatedly. We walked into the room to find out what was going on.

They had nailed the mouthy apprentice to the floor. His shirt and pants were nailed down, all the way to his ankles. They must have used twenty to thirty nails to ensure he could not escape. We laughed our asses off.

"I am calling the cops!" screamed the apprentice repeatedly. "Let me out!"

His face was bright red. We could see how pissed off he was, and we did not care. He deserved it. We all went back to work. He remained nailed to the floor for the next seven hours, whining and shouting threats, which we ignored.

Finally, as we were wrapping up for the day, the head carpenter pulled out the nails. The apprentice jumped to freedom, staring down his superiors like he was about to punch them in the face. The head carpenter gave him his check and told him to leave.

After we finished installing the plumbing, my uncle and I loaded the truck, laughing the entire time. That was a cool day. We loved watching the payback go down.

A REAL SHIT STORM

On a hot summer day, my employer received a call from the owner of a truck stop.

"My septic tank is plugged," he said. "Can you send a crew to come out and fix it?"

The truck stop was a big place, so they sent four of us to do the job. When we arrived, an employee came outside to greet us.

"Welcome!" he said. "The septic tank is somewhere out there."

He pointed to a massive field surrounded by woods.

Most jobs start that way. Customers have no idea where their tanks and pipes are located nor any knowledge of their mechanical systems or processes beyond the toilets. One time it took me twenty minutes to explain to a woman that her toilet was connected to pipes, which ran through the walls into the basement, and then into the sewer. She honestly thought the toilet was free-standing, disconnected from everything, and once she flushed, her crap magically disappeared.

So, it did not surprise me that the truck stop employee had no idea where, amidst the sprawling, gigantic field, the septic tank was located. We walked the grounds searching for it. About eight hundred feet from the building, we saw a hatch.

"Wow!" I exclaimed when we opened it.

It was the largest septic tank I had ever seen. Imagine a large hole in the ground. Five feet down, you see water. Seven feet over, against the wall of the tank, you see the sewer pipe. The entire tank was as big as two truck trailers put together. There was no way for us to put the jet rodder hose into the pipe without sending one of us down into the tank.

Luckily, that day, we had an apprentice on the team. He was about twenty years old and two years into plumbing, which is when most apprentices are eager to prove to their superiors that they know what they are doing.

"I will go down there and push the jet rodder hose into the hole!" he said enthusiastically.

The apprentice threw on the harness, ready to seize his moment. We cranked him down with the rodder. After putting about two-hundred-fifty-feet of the hose into the pipe, he hit the obstruction.

"I got it!" he yelled.

He pushed further to unblock the obstruction. Within seconds, we heard a roar. It sounded like a rush of water echoing in a tunnel, getting closer and closer.

"Get me up! Get me up!" screamed the apprentice.

His voice was high pitched and shaky.

"Hurry! Get me up!" he yelled again.

We rushed to crank him up. The crank, however, did not move quickly enough. The roar grew louder, echoing off the walls of the pipe as it came closer. Suddenly, whoosh! Ten thousand gallons of sewage blasted out, covering the poor apprentice from head to toe. The shit storm was a concoction of bathroom, kitchen and truck wash water, restaurant grease, urine, and crap.

"Mother $%&^*#! #$%&@!" screamed the apprentice, using every cuss word in the book.

We continued cranking him up, which was a bit tougher with shit weighing him down.

The rancid smell permeated every speck of air around us. Although it did not stop us from laughing our asses off. Nothing grossed us out. If I were the one covered in sewage, however, I would have been most bothered by the grease. Cleaning restaurant grease off your body is a terrible experience.

When the apprentice finally reached above ground, he did not say anything. Through his crap-covered face, his eyes glared at us.

"Dude, you volunteered to go down there," I said, trying to defuse the tension. "Oh, and you are riding in the back of the truck."

While that remark did not help pacify his anger, there was no way we were letting that shit covered, stinking kid sit with us during the long ride home.

The truck stop owner never called again. That septic tank remains the biggest one I have ever seen. While you may have expected me to puke from the smell and sight of that concoction of sewage, like I said before, not much gets me sick. The only time I puked on a job was when I pumped a septic tank for a dog kennel at a naval base. The tank was filled to the brim with three thousand gallons of dog shit. I could not stop vomiting. Any human shit storm is more pleasant than a tank of dog shit.

A MOMENT OF REFLECTION

The truth is, while I love plumbing, I wish I was an engineer. When I was a kid, I never knew I could get a student loan and go to college. Those options were not mentioned in my household. My dad expected me to work in a factory like he and his father did. I did not find out about student loans until I was thirty years old.

Plumbing, however, is a great career. My favorite part is figuring out how to get my piping from one point to another, so it looks nice and is out of the way. When you build a system that looks nice, works perfectly, and is not intrusive to the design of the building, it is a pretty cool accomplishment.

The adversity is also interesting. If you cannot laugh at adversity, do not be a plumber. People do not understand why you are ripping out their walls and charging so much money. They do not understand if you move a kitchen sink six inches to the left instead of across the room, it will cost less because we do not have to combat other mechanics. Not to mention, most homeowners prefer to spend money on light fixtures versus plumbing.

There is a pervasive language barrier. Plumbing has its own vocabulary. I must constantly translate plumbing-speak into layman's terms so that the customer understands exactly what I am doing and why I am doing it. I like the challenge, especially when I am explaining to CEOs of huge companies why I need to tear open their walls.

I empathize with customers. How can they understand the more difficult aspects of my trade when they know nothing about it? When my wife talks about bookkeeping, such as making double-entry journals, I nod my head and stare blankly, not understanding a word she is saying. We have been married for twenty years, and I still have not figured it out.

I have one piece of advice. The next time you need a plumber, research the problem ahead of time; otherwise you may end up getting ripped off. One time a guy called me saying a plumber was charging him ten thousand dollars to replace a furnace and air conditioning unit. I called a colleague who charged $5200. The more details you understand about the job, the more you know what it entails and should cost.

CHAPTER 5
KENNY

Plumbing was not my dream career. After graduating college, I landed a job typing school lessons for kids with special needs. I was also a semi-professional comedian, performing stand-up acts at clubs around Canada. Juggling both careers was tough. Not to mention, it was not sustainable financially. I had a longtime girlfriend who I wanted to marry but felt obligated to make more money first, so I could support a family.

Plumbing was my golden opportunity. My grandfather was a plumber. My father is a plumber. So, on a Sunday morning at the breakfast table when I announced my decision to become a plumber, my father cheered with excitement. He needed the help badly. A well-known plumber in the area, who was overwhelmed with calls, asked my father if he would mind taking over some jobs. My father graciously accepted the offer, and his business took off.

Four years later, I am married, leading a successful plumbing career alongside my father.

I am Kenny, and these are my diaries.

METHANE POISONING

My biggest fear as a plumber is getting pink eye. The infection is highly contagious and can spread rapidly from one eye to the next. If one speck of poop splatters into my eye, I could be doomed. Fortunately, on this one call, I did not get pink eye; however I did take home something almost as unpleasant.

One of our regular customers, a restaurant owner, called my father and me, panicking about a clogged toilet.

"You must come now," he said. "Our only toilet is backed up. Something is blocking the drain. Toilet water is spilling onto the basement floor. Please help!"

Normally, my father and I would drop everything to respond to an emergency call; however we were swamped that day with back-to-back emergencies.

"We will come as soon as we can," I said.

"Okay," said the owner. "Please hurry. It is a mess."

While waiting for us, the owner took the problem into his own hands resorting to what was probably the worst temporary fix possible. He went into the basement and opened the drainpipe, which caused the backed-up water, feces, toilet paper, kitchen scraps, and other bodily fluids to release onto the floor.

A couple hours later, my father and I arrived at the restaurant. Since it was later in the afternoon, only a few people were sitting in the dining area, munching on hamburgers and fries.

"Thank you so much for coming," said the owner. "Follow me."

He led us down a steep, rickety staircase into the basement. The pungent smell of methane permeated the room, although it did not bother me. I had smelled much worse odors on other jobs. The floor, on the other hand, was one of a kind. At least three inches of filthy, brown water covered it from wall to wall. Clumps of feces poked their heads above the water. Toilet paper was everywhere. We could not even tiptoe around the mess, leaving us no other option but to step directly in it. Being that I had started my plumbing career only four years prior, I had never encountered that level of gross. I forced my mind to focus on the job as the feces-filled, saturated pool crept around my feet.

The owner stood on the steps the entire time. It was not the first time that toilet had clogged.

"Why does this keep happening? What are we going to do?" he muttered.

"We have to disturb whatever blockage is clogging the drain," I said.

I waded through the sea of excrement, kicking over toilet paper, searching for the floor drain. My father went to the truck to grab our snake and drain machine. A drain machine is a large machine on wheels with a spring-like coil that enters and unclogs the drain. The machine rotates the coil so that it continuously spins as it enters the drain, and either pushes the blockage back into the water or pulls it out. It is a vital piece of plumbing equipment that we use frequently.

When my father returned, we set up the machine. The sea of sewage pooled around its wheels. Once I found the drain, we moved the machine closer to it. My father stood at the top of the machine by the lever, while I stood near the end, next to the coil's tail.

"Let's do this," I said.

My father pulled the lever, and the coil started spinning. Within seconds, I quickly learned I had made a major mistake. I forgot to factor in that a coil rapidly spinning in the middle of dirty water would create backsplash. Drops of water with blips of poop smacked me in the face. I closed my eyes as my body flinched and my stomach turned. Fortunately, I was wearing safety glasses, although one thought continued to swirl inside my head - "Oh no, pink eye!"

"STOP!" I yelled at my father, praying he would hear my voice above the machine's roar.

He heard me. Then again, my shriek was so loud the whole restaurant upstairs may have heard me. My father stopped the machine. Breathing deeply to calm myself down, I wiped the brown speckles off my face. Once I regained my composure, I took a few steps back from the coil, so I would not get blasted in the face again.

"Are you okay?" asked my father.

"Yes," I said. "I am ready. Start it up."

My father pulled the lever. We eventually hit the blockage, which was nothing short of a gargantuan relief. The pool of dirty water flowed down into the drain. It was a beautiful moment until we realized the toilet paper was not flowing anywhere, and it had poop clinging to it. The methane smell did not let up either. Nonetheless, we finished what we were hired to do. The drain was unclogged, and the toilet was working. We packed up our equipment and tip-toed out of there, dodging poop along the way.

A few hours later, while working on another job, a headache overcame me. It was an odd happening considering I never get headaches. Then, I started burping repeatedly. Being that I did not drink anything carbonated, I was not sure what was going on inside my body. Although once I smelled the burps, I figured it out. They smelled like methane. Every time I burped it was like a cloud of methane released into the air, and my headache let up a little bit.

It took five hours for the burping to stop and the headache to go away. A couple months later, the same restaurant owner called again. His toilet was clogged. He needed us to fix it immediately. And off we went.

A DILDO STRIKES AGAIN

A manager of a thirty-year-old residential building in Toronto calls my dad and me regularly. Long ago we became his official "hired plumbers," meaning we were the first plumbers the manager hired, and unless we screw up, we most likely will be the last (until we retire, of course). The building is a modern high rise. Every floor has about twenty units, which gives us plenty of job opportunities. Yet, even after four years servicing the building, I had no idea it had a penthouse unit until we received a call.

"The resident in the penthouse unit is having problems with his washrooms on the main and second floors," said the manager.

"We will be right over," I replied.

My father and I went to the unit and knocked on the door. A guy answered. He looked like he was in his thirties, dressed in jeans and a white t-shirt. He gestured for us to come inside.

"I am the interior designer for this place," he explained, proudly.

The guy clearly knew what he was doing. The place was immaculate. Sculptures stood in every room and hallway. Canvasses covered the walls. Most of the furniture was leather, real leather, not the fake stuff. A glass staircase with wooden handles spiraled up to the second floor.

The designer led us to the washroom on the first floor. We noticed the toilet was not filling up with water at a normal pace.

"It looks like a valve issue," I said. "This is easy to fix."

In ten minutes, we replaced the fill valve with a new one. The designer then led us up the winding staircase to the second floor. Like the rest of the house, the master bedroom was stunning. Abstract art adorned the walls. The furniture had a minimalist look – simple, modern, and chic.

"By the way," said the designer. "I am not the owner of this unit. I am taking care of it for a friend."

He showed us the master bathroom. The walls were made of a beige stone. A large shower with double glass doors stood against the far wall.

"The hot and cold water in the shower are not working," he explained.

"Yet another easy fix," I said.

We simply needed to turn off the valves to shut off the water and replace the cartridge with a new one.

"I need access to the valves," said my father. "Do you know where they are located?"

"No," said the designer. "I do not live here, so I am not sure."

"We need the valves," said my father. "I am opening up everything."

With forceful determination, my father scoured the bathroom, looking for the valves. A feeling of dread came over me. I do not like looking in places customers do not expect us to investigate. Usually, when people know a plumber or other service person is coming into their house, they put away private things that they do not want a stranger to see. Many of our customers go the extra mile and clear cabinets so that pipes and valves are easily accessible.

In our current situation, however, that was not the case. When my father opened the cabinets underneath the sink, everything was there, untouched, including a dildo, which was the size of my forearm. The thing looked angry, like the Pitbull of sex toys. It stared us in the face like it was going to bite us. It even had veins. I had no idea dildos came in that size.

Silence crept across the room. My father, the designer and I stood there, staring at the thing, not quite knowing what to do or say next. The air became so thick, I could not breathe.

Maybe I should have said, "Oh, look at that. That is funny!" or maybe I should have played it cool, pretending like I did not notice it. I felt so uncomfortable, although not because of the sex toy. It was more so because my father and a customer were staring at the sex toy with me. I am typically a champion at handling awkward encounters; however, this dildo took awkward to the next level.

With sweaty palms and my heart pounding, I left the washroom and pretended to admire the art in the master bedroom. After a few minutes, feeling slightly guilty about leaving my father alone in a dildo faceoff, I went back into the bathroom.

My father was crouched down on his hands and knees with his head positioned a tad to the right of the dildo. Even with his face just inches away from it, my father acted like it was not there. The designer stood behind him. I stood off to the side, wishing the entire experience would end soon.

I could not believe how professional my father remained. He looked up and around the dildo as if it were a bottle of cleaning fluid, searching for the valves. At one point, I wondered if he even saw the thing. The search took no more than thirty seconds, yet it felt like it took hours. The silence continued. No one said a word until my father closed the cabinet doors.

"We are going to get our tools," he said, again acting like nothing happened. "We will be back in a bit."

The designer scurried behind us down the staircase.

"Sure, no problem. You know, I do not live here. I am just taking care of the place," he said for the fourth time that day.

I could hear his inner monologue - "This is not my place, and that is not my dildo! Please do not pass judgement on me. It is not mine!"

My father and I left the apartment. We rode the elevator, headed to our truck, and retrieved our tools, in silence. I could not decide if I should say something like, "Sorry, I did not know what to do there," or if I should not say anything. I chose the latter, and so did my father. When we got back into the elevator, I started getting frustrated. My father was either handling himself unbelievably well, or he really did not see it. I had to find out, especially before we went back into the unit.

"Dad," I said. "If you do not have to, I do not think you should go back into that cabinet."

My father blankly stared at the elevator doors. After a few seconds, he turned to me and broke his silence.

"Did you see the size of that thing!?" he exclaimed. "Holy crap! It was huge!"

That was one of my favorite moments. My father is typically a conservative person. I could not believe how professional he remained while knowing a gigantic dildo was nearly touching his face. He locked into work mode, determined to not get weirded out by an experience that rocked his conservative world, let alone with his son standing next to him. I was highly impressed.

We went back inside, replaced the cartridge, and cleaned up our tools. On our way out, my father went a step further trying to lighten the mood.

"You know, you really did a beautiful job designing this place," he said to the designer. "If I ever need an interior designer, I know who to call."

The designer was flattered. Again, I was impressed. After such an awkward experience, my father left on a compliment. It was a heart-warming moment that demonstrated my father's true professionalism.

In a way, plumbers trespass on people's boundaries. Most of us feel safe in the washroom because it is our washroom. We store stuff in there that we do not want nor expect strangers to see until a plumber walks in and needs access to the valves under the cabinet.

We did not receive another call about a problem in the penthouse. We also never needed an interior designer.

A MOMENT OF REFLECTION

I think the most interesting thing about any skilled labor, including plumbing, is that the better you become, the more deceptively easy it looks. Some people will avoid hiring a plumber, insisting they can do the job themselves. Others will hire a plumber and question the cost when they see the bill.

"This job only took you fifteen minutes to complete! How can you charge me this much?" they will ask.

How do I express to that person that the job only took fifteen minutes because I have spent the last seven years doing this work? If it were my first job ever, it would have taken longer; however, because of my extensive experience, the problem is usually something I have seen before and fixed many times.

My favorite customers are those who realize the true value of skilled labor. They will pay me upfront and throw in a tip.

"I really appreciate your work," they will say. "Please have a coffee on me."

Those people make me feel valued.

There is also a power dynamic issue. When I step foot into someone's house, I notice a change in attitude. Some people are welcoming.

"Please, come in," they will say. "Sorry, this place is such a mess. The toilet is over here."

Others act as though they are doing you a favor for letting you come into their home. They sternly talk at you, even though they called you for help. The dynamic is especially prevalent in office buildings where trade workers are essentially treated like intruders.

"You cannot drill at this time," a tenant will say, even though he knows you are doing work for his neighbor down the hall.

"Oh, those bloody plumbers are here," others will mutter under their breath.

No matter how people view what I do, or how unwelcomed some people may make me feel, the bottom line is, good plumbing is a privilege. Plumbers are on the front lines, protecting citizens. Because of plumbers, people have clean drinking water. They can shower and wash dishes with hot water. Indoor plumbing is nonexistent in some parts of the world. People do not have access to clean drinking water. Occasionally, I must remind myself how lucky we are in North America to have quality plumbing.

So even though some people do not understand the value we are providing, when I look at the global picture, I know. Plumbing is honorable work.

CHAPTER 6
ANTHONY

When I was 23 years old, I could not get a regular job. I did not go to college until later in life, which was a mistake. My grandma worked in the plumbing department for the City of Chicago. One day she asked if I wanted to be an apprentice for a plumber who needed assistance.

"Are you crazy, grandma?" I said. "Why would I want to play in someone's toilet?"

A year later, jobs were still tight. I was living with my mom, had two cars, and no gas. I asked my grandma if that plumber still needed an apprentice.

"He moved on," she said. "But I have someone else for you."

My first job was on the South Side of Chicago. We were hired to dig out a trench for a sewer. I expected plumbing to be a temporary gig, hoping to eventually work in a factory. That first job, however, changed my life. Although not because I immediately loved plumbing and wanted to do it forever. A stroke of luck crossed my path while digging out the trench. A few seasoned plumbers were on the job site with me. One of their trucks broke down. The plumber asked if I wanted to earn some extra money by driving him to his next job.

"Sure," I said. "Let's go."

I drove him to his job and stood there, watching him work. The whole thing only took an hour to complete. In return, he gave me one hundred dollars.

"Are we working again tomorrow?" I asked, shocked by how much money I had made in such a short period of time.

"How can someone do this kind of work, for this short of time, and make that much money?" I thought to myself.

That's why I became interested in plumbing. There was no way someone with a high school education could make that much money within an hour or two.

I worked with that plumber for two years, shadowing his every move, learning everything I could about the trade. His bad luck became my good luck, and I am grateful every day for it.

Eight years later, another stroke of good luck headed my way. At that point, I still did not have a plumber's license. I hate to say it, but as a man who is part of the black community, plumbers' licenses are not easy to get. You can be the best plumber out there, know how to do everything, yet contractors will not be interested in giving you a license unless you marry their daughter, or are a nephew. You need a family connection of some sort.

At that time, I had been pulled into a job at a large restaurant chain. We were hired to install all the plumbing. While I was working on-site, an inspector caught me.

"Let's walk through an inspection," he said.

We walked through the whole job.

"I like your work," he said. "But you have to pack up your tools and get out of here."

He was tired of contractors using plumbers without licenses, which for my contractor, was a major problem. His money was tied up. The project had begun. So, he gave me a license.

Today, I am my own contractor, and I also work with other plumbers. The State of Illinois has a limited number of plumbers (only 8,000 I believe), so we all help each other whenever we can.

I am Anthony, and these are my diaries.

DO NOT FORGET TO SPIT

Some people feel comfortable being themselves no matter who they encounter. When I first meet my customers, I make sure to not get in the way of that comfortability. I am not there to criticize them. I just want to get the job done. Nevertheless, people surprise me on a regular basis.

One call I will never forget. My partner and I had been working on an apartment building for quite some time. It contained about twelve units. We were initially hired to replace the stems in the showers because the model was discontinued. We were also asked to check the apartments and follow up on complaints from tenants.

One lady asked that we inspect her dripping bathroom sink. My partner and I knocked on her door. To our surprise, she opened it wearing a black, satin robe, which was about mid-level in length. If she bent over, we would have seen something. She was a middle-aged woman with short, black hair and seemed to be unbothered by her attire. Whenever I am on a job, I try to look people in the eyes and nowhere else. If they feel comfortable wearing nothing but a short robe, I will not make them feel less comfortable having it on by letting my eyes wander. I looked at the woman as if she were my aunt.

"How are you doing?" she said. "Come in. I will show you the sink."

The place was clean. It had three bedrooms and two bathrooms – a master and common bathroom. The lady walked us through the house to the common bathroom off the hallway. The room was tiny. While standing outside the doorway, she pointed to the sink.

"It is leaking under there. I put out a bucket to catch the water," she explained, nodding her head towards a small, white bucket under the sink.

I bent down to look but did not see any water. Nothing was leaking from the pipe, and the bucket was empty.

"This is strange," I thought.

The woman left. The bathroom was so cramped I had to lay on my back to get a closer look under the sink. I shined my flashlight underneath it. My partner ran the water to see if anything started leaking.

A few minutes later, while I was still on my back, holding the flashlight, the woman returned.

"Can you please get out of the way so I can use the sink?" she said to my partner who was standing next to the sink.

He stepped out, confused by the question because I was the one positioned under the sink. She did not say anything to me. Instead, she stood directly over me, her legs straddling my body. I did not know what was going on or what to say. Whatever was happening was crazy, and I did not want to be a part of it. Although I did not have a choice. Her legs trapped me under her. I laid on my back, frozen, forcing my eyes to keep examining the pipes. If I had moved, she might have thought I was trying to peek up her robe. So, I remained still, praying for the moment to pass.

Then she did something completely unexpected. She took out her toothbrush and started brushing her teeth. It seemed like she was putting on a show. She circled the toothbrush in her mouth and moved it back and forth.

Tired of being under her, I wanted nothing more than to get up. I was also nervous. I remembered my teenage years when I was working for a factory, and we learned about sexual harassment. You just do not know how something will come off. I had to remain calm until she left and then get the hell out of there. My partner stood frozen outside the door. He did not know what to do.

After what seemed like hours, the lady finally finished brushing her teeth. When she left the room, I jumped up.

"It is time to go," I said to my partner.

We walked out of the bathroom. The lady was in the kitchen.

"We did not see any leaks," I said.

"That is strange," she said. "I will keep an eye on it."

Once we were outside, my partner started laughing.

"Man," he said. "I wish it were me under the sink! You are so lucky!"

"No, I am not," I replied.

I just wanted to do my job and leave. I am an entrepreneur. I know not to mix business with pleasure, or I will be out another job in addition to facing a possible lawsuit or harassment charges.

That lady was one of many customers who have surprised me during my fifteen years of plumbing. Recently, we had an owner of an apartment building call us. He was an older gentleman and a veteran of the Vietnam War. I had done work for him before. He lived in the basement apartment. Old radios, shoes, hot plates, records, and other junk covered the floor.

He called us this time because the basement was flooded. When we arrived, he opened the door.

"Hey," he said. "Let me take you back there to show you from where you can rod."

We walked through the front of the building, down into his basement apartment. Blackish, gray, grease-like slush blanketed the floor. It smelled nasty. Most plumbers will tell you that grease smells worse than wastewater. It was disgusting. In the lowest part of the basement, the slush came up to our ankles. Further away from the floor drains, it covered the soles of our shoes.

Fortunately, we were wearing boots. After so many years of plumbing, we also had strong stomachs. If you are squeamish about smells, the job will take all day. We learn to ignore the smell and protect ourselves by wearing gloves, eyewear, long sleeves, and sometimes masks. If waste splashes into our mouths, we clean it off with peroxide, alcohol, soap, or whatever it takes. If waste splashes into our face and we are not wearing a mask, we joke about "tasting the rainbow." You must protect yourself.

The man walked us through the slushy, greasy mess, and opened a basement door, which led to the backyard. While standing outside, we looked down and could not believe what we saw.

The man was barefooted. He walked through that filthy, slushy grease pond sans socks and shoes. It was nasty, and his feet looked disgusting. They were thick, puffy, and mangled. Walking barefooted in that kind of mess was just something you do not do.

While I wanted to ask, "Hey man, where are your shoes?" I did not ask that question. There are things we see on jobs that we do not discuss out loud with the customer. If we do, we risk scaring off money. We never want to scare off money. If it makes sense and the moment is right, we say something. In this case, however, we did not say a word.

We rodded the sewer, cleaned the water out of the basement, and left.

THE WOMAN WHO STUCK AROUND…FOREVER

On a chilly, winter evening, my buddy called me. He was at a woman's house, hanging out with a group of musicians.

"Hey man, come over here right now," he said. "Put down everything you are doing and come over here. I want you to unclog this drain for these people."

It was 9 p.m. The thought of getting off my couch, going to someone's house and unclogging a drain did not appeal to me that late at night.

"I cannot come over," I said. "I am tired. I do not feel like working. I cannot do it."

"Man, come over here!" he pleaded. "Please look at this job."

"Ugh, fine," I said. His begging made me cave.

The house was in a quiet, residential neighborhood. A line of cars was parked along the driveway. I knocked on the door with my flashlight in-hand. My buddy answered.

"Hey man," he said, with a big smile on his face. "Thank you for coming over so quickly. Come inside."

About fifteen people, including several beautiful women, were hanging out in the living room. Some were playing cards; others were talking.

"Hey," said my buddy. "This is the lady who rents the house. She wants to show you the drain."

He pointed to a pretty, light-skinned girl standing across from him. She wore blue jean shorts and a pink t-shirt, which showed off her belly. Her hair was long and dark and had streaks in it.

"What is the problem?" I asked.

Since she was so pretty, most guys would have been nervous to talk to her, however not me. When I talk about plumbing, my mind drifts somewhere else. Plumbing puts me in my comfort zone. I can focus on it no matter who is standing in front of me, and I am confident talking about it because I know the trade so well.

"Follow me," said the girl.

She walked me through the house, into the kitchen.

"This sink is clogged," she said, pointing to the kitchen sink, which was filled with water.

"I am sorry, but I cannot fix this tonight," I told her, tiredly. "If you can get someone else to come here tonight, great. If not, I can come by in the morning. I just cannot work this late at night."

To my relief, she understood.

"Okay," she said. "Let me get your number. You can come back and do the job."

I gave her my number and left. The next day, I showed up at 10 a.m. A few ladies from the night before were still there hanging out. The girl welcomed me inside and walked me to the kitchen.

"Go ahead. Please take care of it," she said, pointing to the sink. She then went upstairs.

I crouched down underneath the sink and unclogged the drain. The blockage was not anything serious, just food along with some grease. Since it was a newer house, it had a PVC line, which was easy to open. Older homes have cast iron pipes, which get rusty inside. Those clogs are harder because, after some time, the water and grease sit in the belly of the pipe and harden the inside.

The entire job took me less than thirty minutes.

"I am done!" I shouted.

"I'll be down in a minute!" she yelled from upstairs.

I stood near the front door, waiting for her. The other ladies surrounded me, asking all kinds of questions about how and why I became a plumber.

After a few minutes, the girl came downstairs. She gave me my money, and I left.

I assumed I would never see her again, however one week later she called.

"Do you remember me?" she asked.

I did not recognize her number.

"No," I replied. "Who are you?"

"You came over to my house and unclogged the sink. Remember?"

"Oh, yeah," I said.

"I need you to do something else," she said.

"Oh, yeah?" I asked.

"I did not notice it that day, but there is a hole in my living room wall," she explained. "It must have happened during the party. Do you know anyone who can fix it, or can you fix it?"

"Yeah, I can come over," I replied.

While fixing holes was not part of my plumbing portfolio, I knew a guy who could help. We went to the girl's house. When she opened the door, my buddy's jaw dropped to the floor.

"Oh my gosh! She does not even have to pay me," he whispered as she let us inside.

"No," I softly replied. "You have to get paid to do the work."

"Are you sure?" he asked.

"Yes," I said.

"Oh man! Are you sure?" he asked one more time.

"Dude," I said, slightly irritated. "You came here to make some money. She called and needed a job done. We gotta get paid!"

The job took two hours. He patched the wall and made it look nice. Pleased with his work, the girl paid us, and we left.

"How did you meet her?" asked my buddy once we were outside. He then proceeded with many follow up questions.

After that day, I thought I would never see the girl again. One week later, however, she called.

"Can you take me to the grocery store?" she asked.

"Take you to the grocery store?" I replied, with obvious skepticism in my voice.

"I will pay you," she said.

Considering she lived close to my mom's house, it seemed like an easy way to make money. I picked her up and dropped her off at the store.

"Do you want to come with me or stay here?" she asked before closing the car door.

"I will wait here," I replied.

During that time, in addition to plumbing, I had a second job working as a set-up technician at a plant that made transmission screens. Since I had to be at work at 3 p.m. that afternoon, I could not sit in a grocery store parking lot all day.

An hour and a half later, the girl finally emerged from the store. I drove her home, and she paid me fifty dollars in cash.

"Man, this is nice," I thought. "Here is this nice-looking woman and she is giving me money. Oh wow!"

I expected her to call me again after that day; however I did not hear from her.

"Oh man, what happened to her?" I thought, a bit worried.

After several days of hoping she would call, I decided not to think about it anymore. A month later, to my pleasant surprise, she called again.

"Do you want to come with my friends and me to hang out at a club?" she asked.

"Hang out at a club?" I replied, wondering why she wanted me there.

"Yeah," she said. "I will pay your cover charge to get into the club and pay for anything you want when we are there. I just need you to drive my girls and me."

While I am not a frequent club-goer, this opportunity would cost me nothing, and I would get a free drink out of it, so I agreed to join them.

"Alright, cool," I said.

Around 10 p.m. that night, I drove the girl and her three friends to a hole-in-the-wall club on the South Side. The club looked like a speakeasy. We knocked on the non-descript door. A bouncer opened it a crack. We stated our names, and he let us inside. I felt way out of my element.

After a few hours of hanging out, I drove the girl and her friends back to my house. They got in their car and drove off.

I spent a few more months driving her and her friends to clubs. Each time, she would pay my cover charge and buy me whatever I wanted that night. At one point, she moved into a new house and gave me a key.

"I am going out of town for ten days," she said. "This is the key to my new place. Can you check on it from time to time?"

"I guess so," I said.

Two weeks later, she asked me to give back the key.

"I have a new boyfriend," she said. "I will need my key back."

That was when I figured it out. She was crushing on me, and I had no idea the entire time. I am not the best at picking up on hints. I was also very focused on making money.

It did not matter anyway. She kept me as a friend.

Eight years later, we got married.

ONE EYE DANNY

Some people see money before they see safety. In my early years as a plumber, I knew this guy, Danny. He was a plumber, too and addicted to heroin. Danny was mid-height, about five foot eight, and light-skinned. He had a slim build and black hair which he tied up in a pigtail. For years, I tried helping him get clean. When he lost his van, I drove him to the methadone clinic. No matter how hard he tried, however, he could not overcome the addiction.

One summer, a lady hired us to install hot and cold-water pipes in an apartment building on the South Side. It was a big, brick building, with balconies on each floor and an entry gate to which I had the keys. No one had been living in it yet.

The streets around the building were busy with people looking for money and drugs. They would do just about anything to get their fix and played games with plumbers and contractors because they knew we had money. If we were not careful, they could steal my copper or stealthily take money out of my pocket. In the worst-case scenario, they could stick me up. If any of us had a naïve mindset, they would use it to their advantage.

Since Danny was working on the building with me, people approached the entry gate all the time asking for him because they wanted drugs. One time, when he was not there, a lady approached the gate. She was an older, brown-skinned lady. She was not wearing dingy or dirty clothing, like most people may expect drug addicts to wear. She wore clean, nice clothes and walked and talked slowly.

"Where is the guy?" she shouted over the gate. I knew she was talking about Danny.

"He is not here," I shouted back.

"Can you let me in?" she asked. "I want to come in the building, sit down and talk to you," she said.

"No," I replied. "I have work to do."

No matter what she said, I was not going to let her tempt me. I continued working, ignoring her comments until she left.

A couple hours later, a guy came by. He was wearing faded jeans and a white t-shirt.

"Is Danny here?" he shouted over the gate.

"Nope," I replied.

"Do y'all need help working on anything? Do you mind if I come around? I can help clean up," he said.

They always asked to help work on jobs; however, only half of them really wanted to work. That half would do anything you wanted if it meant drug money was coming. They became the nicest people in the world. Some would even do your work for you.

"You gotta ask my boss," I said to the guy. "He is not here."

"Can I get his number?" he asked.

"You gotta catch him over here," I said. "He will be back around four or five. Or, come in the morning."

The guy left. Turned out, attracting drug addicts and thieves to our job sites was not the worst of Danny's problems.

On a hot, summer day, a plumbing contractor called.

"I need you to go to the east side of the city," he said. "There is a two-flat over there. I need you to dig up the ground so we can install a sewer pipe from the building to the street. I had another guy on the job; however he unexpectedly left. Can you go?"

Building owners like to see at least one plumber or contractor always working on the job because that indicates their money is in motion.

"Sure," I replied. "I will head that way."

Two days prior to starting the job, during a heavy rainfall, a water main broke next to the building. Water flooded the street. City crews dug up the ground to fix it. The street was a sloppy mess. Unlike the west side of the city, where the ground is made of clay, on the east side, the ground is made of sand. The city crews scrambled to fix the water main quickly because if sand got caught inside the line, it would terminate the potable drinking water.

When I arrived, sand was everywhere, covering every speck of the ground. It looked like a beach in the middle of a residential neighborhood. I could not even use my backhoe because of all the sand. My only option was to dig out a trench with a shovel. A guy helped me for a little bit. After thirty minutes, however, he left. Because the water main break created such a disaster, the electrical company showed up to mark the ground. They wanted to spray paint indicators to show me, and any other plumbers who may work on the job, where the utilities were located. That way, we knew where it was safe to dig.

Because there was so much sand, however, the electrician could not spray paint the ground nor, at the very least, install flag indicators. He gave me a verbal warning instead.

"There is an electrical vault in the ground," he said. "Whatever you do, do not go through it. You can go above it and below it, but not through it."

"We have different people working on this site," I said.

"Everyone should know there is an electrical vault in the ground," he replied. "Spread the word."

When we trenched the sewer, we could see the vault. It was made of brick and extended through the entire block.

The next day, the contractor stopped by the site. I told him about the vault and emphasized repeatedly that he should pass the word on to everyone who was working on the job. I spent the rest of the day digging, avoiding the vault.

The next day was Sunday. The contractor called me.

"Can you go back to the site?" he asked. "There is more digging to do."

After six days of digging out the sewer line, I was exhausted.

"Sorry, man." I replied. "I cannot do it today. I need to rest."

My buddy and Danny went to the site instead. I assumed the contractor told them about the vault. I told them about it too, just in case.

My buddy told me that Danny seemed off like he was on drugs. He took out a chipping gun and started chipping away at the brick on the outside of the vault.

"Hey man, we can go straight into this brick," Danny told my buddy.

Boom! Seconds later, the vault exploded. My buddy told me he saw an arch of light. Sparks were everywhere. Danny fell lifeless into the hole. Rocks and sand clung to his face. My buddy raced over to Danny and carried him out of the hole. The contractor stood nearby, frozen with fear.

Danny made it out alive; however he lost an eye. Work slowed down significantly after that day. Lawyers repeatedly knocked on my door, took me to lunch, and asked me questions. They wanted to learn more about our safety policies.

"Do you have to wear eye gear, safety vests, and helmets?" they asked.

Danny filed lawsuits although he did not win any of them because of his past record. He made some poor choices as an addict, which led to encounters with law enforcement. He is lucky he did not lose his life that day. If he had a clear head and listened to the warning about the vault, assuming the contractor gave him one, the explosion would not have happened.

TASTING THE RAINBOW

After a year of plumbing, feeling squeamish on jobs goes out the window. I always thought I was immune to everything, at least almost everything.

Eight years ago, I worked on a job that will be etched in my memory for eternity. A friend's wife called. She ran a property management company. One of her houses had a clogged drain.

"Can you go over to the house?" she asked, urgently. "The tenant is there. The drain is clogged. Can you do it today?"

"Yes, I can do it today," I replied.

It was a bitterly cold, winter morning. Not knowing if I would be working outside, I wore my warm, insulated overalls. The house was small, one-level (not including the basement) and made of brick. When I knocked on the door, an elderly lady opened it.

"Hey, young man," she said with a warm smile.

"Hello. What is going on with the house?" I asked.

"The drain is clogged. The water kept coming out of the toilet, so I unplugged the sump pump," she explained.

She knew what she was doing. When the drain is clogged, if the pump is on, it pushes wastewater to other openings in the house. By unplugging the pump, she prevented the water from flooding the basement, although it did end up flooding a bathtub in the house's only bathroom.

Standing in her doorway, I smelled a hint of sewage. The woman gestured for me to walk further inside. Her husband sat silently on the couch, letting his wife do all the talking. She led me to the basement, which was dry, fortunately. I found the sewer system. It was about as high as my abdomen and stuck out from the wall.

"Is there another cleanout outside?" I asked.

"Yes," she said.

We went upstairs and out the back door. I saw a white pipe sticking out of the ground. It had a cap on it. When I walked over to it, the woman left. I do not blame her for wanting to go inside. It was so cold; I could see my breath in the air.

I decided to take the cap off the outside pipe versus the one inside. That way if sewage water spurted out, it would spill outside, instead of flooding the basement floor. I called my friend's wife to give her an update.

"I can do the job," I said and gave her the price.

"Okay," she said. "Go do it."

I went to my truck to get my tools, which included a Channellock (that is like a plier) and a rodder. I clenched the Channellock around the cap of the pipe and tried twisting it. Man, it was one tough cap! I kept clenching, trying to twist harder and harder. It would not budge. I threw my body weight into it, clenching and twisting harder. Finally, after one final yank, the nut came off. Pow! Wastewater shot in my face and into my mouth.

"Ahhhhhh!" I screamed. "It got in my mouth!"

Disgusted, I began to panic. The wastewater hit me so fast, I did not even see the color, although I knew fully well feces and urine were in that line. Horrified I ingested it, I kept spitting and spitting. I must have spit out every drop of saliva in my body. I ran to my truck and called a friend's mom, who was a nurse.

"I am so grossed out!" I shrieked. "The wastewater went into my mouth!"

I felt like I was going crazy. My head spun. My body shook. My heart raced.

"It is going to be okay, Anthony," said my friend's mom, soothingly. "If you get sick, just come in."

I always keep peroxide in my truck. I poured some in my mouth and rubbed it on my face.

"Oh my gosh! I do not want to get messed up by this stuff," I thought.

My mind spiraled. I remembered I had a Tetanus shot earlier that year, which calmed me down a little bit.

Inside the house, the woman must had heard me yelling.

"Oh shit, my mouth!" I exclaimed as she opened the front door.

"What is going on?" she asked.

"Wastewater came up. It sprayed me in the face and got in my mouth!" I shouted.

"So sorry to hear that. Baby, do you want some bottled water?" she asked calmly.

"Yes!" I cried.

I called my friend's wife and told her what happened.

"I do not want to do this job anymore," I said, hoping she would tell me to go home.

I felt disgusting. All I wanted was mouthwash, soap, and a hot shower.

"Please!" she begged. "Please, stay and do the job. They are good tenants."

"Ugh," I grunted.

Inside my head, I was blaming her for what happened.

"It will cost you extra if I stay," I said.

"Okay, fine," she replied.

I pulled myself together. The worst had already happened. I had to move on and unplug the drain. Driven to finish the job and get the hell out of there, I jammed my rodder into the line to clean it out. The job took about thirty minutes. I felt frustrated the entire time, desperately wanting to leave. To be honest, I probably did a half-ass job. I did not feel like myself.

The minute I arrived at my house later that afternoon, I scrubbed my clothes, body, hair, and mouth. Thankfully, I did not get sick; however I feared a similar episode happening again. So, from that day on whenever I opened a drain, I wore a mask.

I guess it was my turn to taste the rainbow.

THE PLUMBERS OF ILLUSIONED HAZARD

It was a hot, sticky, summer day. A family friend called me about a job.

"Someone needs a rod job," she said. "Are you interested?"

Work had been slow that week. I needed the extra money badly.

"Yes," I said.

"Okay," she said. "Go over there and check it out."

I asked my plumber friend, Joe, to come with me. He needed the money too. The building was on the north side. It looked like a big, old church. It was made of brick and had two floors. We knocked on the door. A woman answered. She was about five feet eight inches tall with brown skin and short hair. She looked to be in her late thirties.

"What do you want?" she asked, suspiciously.

"We are the plumbers," I said. "We were called to help you. What is the problem?"

"Come in," she said, opening the door wider for us to go inside.

The place was full of women. They were casually chatting, holding meetings, beading, and playing games. They filled every corner of every room. I did not see one man in the entire house.

"What is this place?" I thought to myself.

"Our kitchen line is clogged," said the woman, as she walked us through the house into the shared kitchen. "We need it unclogged."

"Okay," I said. "We just bought this new rodder specifically for kitchen lines. We cannot wait to use it."

The kitchen was large. It had three sinks, one of which was flooded with water, and multiple rectangular counters for preparing meals.

Following our usual protocol for jobs like this one, Joe and I looked around the building to inspect the drains. There was an overhead drain in the basement and a catch basin in an outside courtyard. Since the catch basin did not have any water in it, we knew the blockage had to be where the drain went out in the basement, not in the kitchen sink.

We headed into the basement and spotted a two-way cleanout, which was the perfect place to insert our rodder because if we had to release water, it would flow onto the basement floor instead of into the kitchen. We went to our truck, retrieved the rodder, and went back into the building. On our way to the basement, we saw a sign on the wall with an acronym on it that we did not recognize.

Back in the basement, we put on our rubber gloves and started rodding. Joe did the hands-on work, pushing the rodder while I pushed down the pedal. In those days, we did not have self-feeding rodders like we have now. We had to push the rodder with our hands. It would spin, and then we had to push it again. Joe and I talked and joked as we worked like we always did.

"Hey, did you see that sign on the wall?" asked Joe.

"Yeah, I saw it," I replied.

What do you think that acronym means?" asked Joe.

He was always curious about everything. Whenever we went on jobs, he paid attention to every little detail. He was that kind of guy – always asking questions, talking, and looking around.

"Why are there so many women here?" he asked further. "We have not seen one man in the whole place."

I did not have answers for him. When I am on a job, I am focused on the job. I do not pay attention to anything else. Although I was slightly curious about why so many women lived in the building.

After twenty minutes of rodding, the woman came down to check on us.

"How are you guys doing?" she asked.

"We are okay. We should be done in a minute," I said. "We hit a bad spot, but I think it should be alright."

"What does that acronym mean on the sign on the wall?" asked Joe. He could not help himself. He needed an answer.

"This is a home for women who have HIV and AIDS," she explained and walked away.

Joe froze like a statue. The blood drained from his face. He did not say a word. After a few minutes, he broke from the trance and grabbed a bucket of bleach standing nearby (we always bring bleach to kitchen line jobs in case we need to clean up). He poured the entire bucket all over his body.

"What the hell?" I asked.

The woman's response surprised me, however not to the point of dousing myself with bleach. The kitchen line did not have any blood in it, just grease and food, which were not harmful.

Joe would not stop freaking out. He repeatedly rubbed the bleach all over his body. He poured it on his arms, hands, and shoulders. I thought he was having a nervous breakdown.

"Man, can you please take me home?" he asked, pleading with me to get out of there.

The woman paid us more money than we usually made for that kind of job. On the way home, Joe, who is usually a live wire, talking and laughing every minute, was a man of few words.

He ended up fine, of course; however the experience reinforced my obsession with protecting myself on jobs. While not in that case, plumbers are at risk of engaging with hazardous substances, some of which are unknown. That is the scary part about plumbing. Whenever I go to a job, I always wear long sleeves, gloves, eyewear and sometimes a mask, depending on what I am doing.

Safety is everything when it comes to plumbing or any construction job. If you do not prioritize safety, you will not have a career for very long.

A MOMENT OF REFLECTION

I never imagined plumbing would be my lifelong career. Like I said earlier, when my grandma first mentioned the idea to me, I thought she was crazy. I refused to play in people's toilets. Desperate for cash; however, I took that one job, and here I am today. I plan to be a plumber for the rest of my life. My business is so strong that customers call me regularly and give me referrals.

One day, tired of the phone ringing off the hook, I declared I was going to quit plumbing.

"I cannot take it anymore," I said to myself. "I am going to quit!"

Strangely, almost immediately after making that statement, the phone stopped ringing.

"Dang!" I thought. "I have not worked in a week! What happened?"

The next thing I knew the phone started ringing again. From that day forward, I promised I would never say I am going to quit.

Plumbing is reliable work. If the economy turns and everyone is laid off from their jobs, I can still earn a living. People will always call because they always need a plumber. And once they find that plumber, barring a significant mishap, most customers stick around. Some of my customers' grandkids are now my customers. I will be old and hunched over, and they will still be calling me because I am their guy. They can trust me to get the job done.

I am currently teaching my younger brother the art of plumbing. He is 27-years-old. I started training him two years ago because I needed help on jobs, and he needed money. It was the perfect fit. Sometimes if you do not have someone watching your back on certain jobs, bad things can happen.

I had a friend who was called to a job in a condominium building. He wanted me to go with him; however the condominium owner said she did not want to pay extra money for an extra person. People always try to cut corners to save money.

Following the owner's orders, my friend went to her condo alone to change a valve. When he arrived, he mistakenly thought the valve was turned on and ended up flooding the entire unit. Water poured onto the floors, couch, new flat screen television, and other furniture. If I had been there, I would have spotted his mistake and prevented the disaster.

The two most important lessons I have learned as a plumber are to make sure you are working safely (as I learned the hard way when the raw sewage shot into my mouth), and that you have help when you need it.

CHAPTER 7
ANDY

When I turned 32-years-old, I knew I needed a change. I had been feeding veal calves for eleven years. It was the same routine every day, and I worked long hours. Tired of the monotony, I looked for jobs where every day brought new challenges and experiences.

My dad owned an excavating business. I joined him from time to time, putting together pipes. The skills I acquired while working on projects were easily transferable to plumbing, so when a job at a plumbing company opened in town, I applied and got it.

I felt proud to become part of a well-respected trade. I received my plumbing certification, worked at that company for twelve years, and then started my own shop.

Back in my veal feeding days, I never imagined one day I would be a plumber, let alone a business owner. Three decades later, business is booming, and I enjoy every minute of it.

I am Andy, and these are my diaries.

THE UNEXPECTED BUNKMATE

I take care of many rental buildings, most of which are filled with college students. The work is steady and interesting. Renters do not seem to care who is in their personal space, even if it means getting in bed with them.

On a chilly fall day, a landlord called. He needed me to remove air conditioner units from one of his rental buildings. He hired me every year for this job, so I knew the property well. It was a two-story house, which was divided into apartments. From one year to the next, I never knew who was living there. College students move around a lot.

My assistant and I went to the first apartment and knocked on the door. A young woman answered.

"I am here to take out the air conditioner unit," I explained.

She gestured for us to come inside. The apartment had three bedrooms. The air conditioner unit was installed in the window of one of the rooms. I knocked on the bedroom door.

"We are the plumbers," I said loudly. "We are here to remove the air conditioner unit in your bedroom."

"Come in," a woman's voice mumbled.

She sounded like she had just woken up (at noon. Ah, college life). I opened the door to find a young woman lying in bed, clutching the covers which were pulled up to her chin. The bed was against the window where the air conditioner unit was installed.

"Hi, I am Andy, the plumber," I explained, feeling a bit awkward talking to a twenty-something-year-old who I was meeting for the first time, as she laid in bed.

"I need to remove that air conditioner unit from your window. I can come back later if this is a bad time."

"No, no. Please do it now," she insisted, yet remained in bed.

"Uh, I need access to that air conditioner unit next to your bed. Uh, this seems like a bad time. I can come back later," I said.

"Please, get out of bed!" my inner voice screamed.

My assistant, who was an older fellow, stood there silently. He did not know what to do. We looked at the young woman. She stared back at us.

"No, no, no. Do not come back. Just do it now," she repeated, pulling the covers tighter and staying in bed.

"You have got to be kidding me," I thought, hoping no one was taking pictures.

"Well, I have to get right there," I said, pointing to the window directly above her bed.

She did not respond.

With no other option, I climbed in bed with her. I propped my body on top of her legs and started removing the unit. My stomach pressed against her thighs. It was extremely uncomfortable, at least for me.

"How long will you be here?" she asked.

"Not very long," I said, thinking I had to get out of there, quickly.

I was in bed with her for at least ten minutes. I took out the screws, removed parts, and pulled out the unit. She continued laying there, unbothered by an unknown man on top of her in bed.

Once the unit was out, I pushed myself back up.

"Thanks," I said.

"Hey, no problem!" she exclaimed like it was just another day.

When my assistant and I got back to the truck, we could not stop laughing. I had been on jobs where residents answered the door naked, or in their underwear. Never had someone gotten that intimate with me. That job was one of a kind.

College kids play by a different set of rules, which is usually no rules. I frequently work in women's restrooms on college campuses. Even when I put up the ribbon and "do not enter" sign, women come in and use the bathroom next to where I am working. I was in a restroom the other day that had showers. Three women walked right past me, as if I were invisible, with their towels wrapped around their bodies, ready to take a shower. Of course, it did not bother me. I went about my business, pretending not to notice. After all, in plumbing, things could always be worse.

THE VAGINAL SURPRISE

One of my regular customers is a landlord who owns a bunch of rental homes. The homes are large with eight or nine bedrooms. He converted most of them into apartments, which gave me a continuous stream of jobs. The landlord lived out of state. Every now and then, he would pop in and hire me to do maintenance on the homes. One of those homes was a two-story, old brick house. It had four apartments, two on the main floor and two upstairs.

"Can you meet me at the house?" he asked during one of his visits. "I want to walk you through some electrical and plumbing stuff I need done."

While my main trade is plumbing, I work on electrical jobs too. For many of my customers, I am a human Swiss Army Knife.

"Sure, I will meet you there," I said.

It was a Sunday afternoon. I arrived at the house first. The place looked empty. Not one car was parked in the driveway or along the street. A few minutes later, the landlord showed up.

"Hi Andy," he said. "Good to see you again. I have some drawings here I want to show you."

He pulled out a notepad filled with drawings of the projects he wanted me to work on in some of the apartments. We walked around the house as he explained the priority list of which jobs were most important. We had keys to the house and all the apartments. Almost all the tenants were not home, as I expected. The ones who were there acted like we were invisible, which is not surprising in this line of work.

From the entryway, we made our way up a circling wooden staircase that was painted white and falling apart. At the top, apartment units three and four were to our right and left. We knocked on unit four's door. The resident was not home, so we let ourselves inside. I knew the unit well; however the renters changed frequently. The current resident was a single guy, and it was clear he did not have a housekeeper. Video games and movies were scattered everywhere. Dirty dishes piled high in the kitchen sink. A half-eaten sandwich sat on the counter. I assessed the kitchen faucet and drain, which were on the repair list. I then moved onto the bathroom. It looked like I had remembered it – small, with white porcelain tile and fixtures. I had installed the toilet, shower and sink five years prior. I remembered taking down the whole ceiling to install new plastic pipes and water lines.

The landlord stood next to me, pointing out things that needed fixing. We stood shoulder-to-shoulder looking up and down. We took two steps to our right to reach the bathtub, which was also a shower. I pulled back the curtain to check if the faucet was leaking. And then I saw them.

"What the heck is that?" I thought, although did not say out loud.

I could not figure out if the landlord, who was still standing next to me, saw them too. Considering he was looking in the tub at my same angle, it would have been nearly impossible for him to miss them.

Two sex toys – a giant strap-on dildo and fake vagina – were placed side-by-side on the floor of the tub. The dildo looked to be about ten inches long. The fake vagina was a beige, skin-like color. I could not stop staring at it, although not because I found it attractive. I just could not believe that kind of toy existed. I had never seen anything like it.

The landlord did not move, nor say anything about them. He kept talking about the job and work that needed to be done. Not hearing a word, I continued staring at the toys for what seemed like forever.

When the landlord stopped talking, I snapped out of my trance, shut the shower curtain, and slowly backed out of the room. We left the apartment, locked the door and went back outside. Dildos and fake vaginas floated around my head as the landlord explained more about the job. He never said anything about them.

When I got home that night, I told my wife about the discovery.

"I found a giant dildo and some other fake vagina-type toy that a guy would wear between his legs," I explained.

She burst out laughing. She had a name for the fake vagina, but I do not remember it now. We both had a good laugh that night.

A SEA OF SEWAGE

I clean a lot of sewers. I have a sewer machine, camera, and an excavator, so I am ready for the worst of the worse, which came in handy on one job.

A man called me about a plugged sewer. He, his wife and two young kids lived in a two-story home. I had been there before and remembered the house was filthy. A job is a job, however, so I told him I would be right over and brought my 11-year-old son with me.

When I knocked on the door, the man answered.

"The sewer is plugged," he said. "Nothing flushes. I think something is wrong in the basement."

My son and I went inside. Filthy was an understatement. Piles of dog poop were scattered across the floor. Dog and cat hair blanketed everything. Clothes hung off every piece of furniture. Dirty dishes piled high in the sink to the point where they blocked the window above it. The kitchen floor looked like it had never been cleaned. Food stains stuck to the tile with a thick layer of pet hair covering them. The whole house reeked of poop, even in the kitchen. With or without the plugged sewer, I am certain it always smelled like that.

My son followed me, his mouth hanging open the entire time. It was his first time seeing a home that dirty. I, on the other hand, had seen many of them, some of which were even worse.

We opened the basement door and started descending an old wooden staircase. About halfway down, I stuck out my arm to block my son from moving any further.

"Stop," I said, squinting a bit to decipher the situation below us. "What the heck is that?"

My son peeked out from behind my shoulder. He could not figure it out either.

"Stay right there," I said. "I am going to check it out."

I walked down further to get a closer look. A sea of sewage flooded the basement. It looked like the line broke weeks prior. I would need to wade through the mess to reach the line.

"Wait here," I said to my son, who stood frozen on the steps. "I am going to the truck."

I put on my boots and walked back downstairs. Smells usually do not bother me on jobs; however this was close to the worst smell I had ever encountered. A basement window was broken enabling some fresh air to flow inside, although it was not nearly enough. The room was small, which squeezed the sewage into a confined space, making the smell and depth even worse.

I waded into the sea. To my right, I saw a second room. I glided towards it. The sewage weighed down my boots, making it difficult to move, and it got deeper the further I trudged. When I reached the room, I froze in disbelief. A washer, dryer and two and a half feet of clothes were floating in sewage. It was disgusting. I could not believe the homeowners were living like this, let alone with kids.

The broken part of the sewage pipe was near the top of a side wall, which made it easy to repair. The section of the pipe on the outside of the house was made of clay. The section inside was made of cast iron. The iron and clay merged along the wall inside the house, which is where the breakage occurred. The clay tile broke, so I ran a new piece of pipe from the outside, through the wall, into the basement and reconnected it with the cast-iron section.

After finishing the job, my son and I went back upstairs.

"It is fixed," I said to the owners, who were casually sitting on the stained couch watching television.

"Your basement is full of sewage. Your washer, dryer, and piles of clothes are floating in it," I explained further.

They looked at me with a blank stare.

"Do you want me to remove the sewage?" I asked.

"No," they said in unison.

Relieved, my son and I bolted before they had a chance to change their minds. I assumed they cleaned up the sewage themselves or at least hoped so.

"I do not know how you can do stuff like that, dad," said my son as we drove home.

He ended up working with me when he got a little older, so that day would not be the first time he would see a sea of sewage. Crap-covered basements are commonplace in my business. In fact, not long after that job, another customer called me about a similar problem.

The homeowners, two middle-aged women, said their sewer was plugged. It was pouring rain that day. The town had a combination drainage system, meaning the sewage and rainwater drained out of the same place. If it rained a lot, it overloaded the sewer system. Knowing the overload happened frequently, I called the city before going to the women's home.

"I am about to inspect a home," I explained. "The sewer is plugged. Before I go, will you please check the city sewer outside their home to make sure it is not plugged?"

If the city sewer was plugged, the private sewer would also be plugged. The city sent a crew to check the sewer. They said it was fine.

With that question answered, I went to the house. It was a two-story home. I knew it well because I had worked on electrical jobs there before. I brought an assistant with me. He was an older gentleman who had recently retired from his full-time job. When we arrived at the house, one of the women came to the door.

"I have to put the dogs away," she said. "Please go around to the side door."

We walked around to a side door in the alley. She let us inside, walked us through the kitchen and down the steps into the basement. We brought our equipment with us – the sewer machine, boots, gloves, and other tools.

It was a large basement, about thirty by forty feet. The women owned a book shop. Books of all sizes were piled high on shelves and stacked in boxes around the room. We saw sewage leaking from the cleanout cap, which is meant to prevent leaks. Alarm bells rang inside my head. I knew something was seriously wrong.

We removed the cleanout cap, grabbed a bucket, filled it with the seeping sewage, and dumped it in the yard. The sewage kept coming. The smell permeated the room as the brown liquid stained our gloves. One bucket was not enough.

"We need to move faster," I said to my assistant. "Grab another bucket."

We filled the buckets one by one, catching most of the sewage. Some of it escaped, however, and dripped onto the floor. After filling thirty buckets, I realized the sewage was not slowing down. We had been there for an hour and a half catching it.

"We are not getting anywhere," I said to my assistant.

"Yeah, seems like there is a bigger problem," he replied.

I went upstairs and explained the situation to the homeowners.

"Sorry, but we are not making headway. The sewage will not stop coming out," I said. "We need to pull out the cap entirely, let it go, and see how much sewage we can collect."

"Is that the only solution?" asked one of the women.

I understood her hesitation. Pulling the cap meant running the risk of flooding the basement with sewage.

"That is our only option," I said. "I cannot bucket this all night long."

They gave me the green light. I went back downstairs and told my assistant to pull the cap. Feces and water gushed out of the four-inch-round pipe, spilling onto the floor. It kept coming and coming, pooling around our feet. The entire floor was covered, except for one little corner. The owners watched from the steps. Their eyes nearly popped out of their heads, and their mouths hung open.

"How long will that run?" asked one of them.

"Until it empties out your sewer," I replied, feeling sorry for them.

No one enjoys watching someone's basement flood with feces, especially one that had such a massive collection of books.

Finally, after the sewage reached about four inches deep, it stopped. Knowing the problem went beyond their sewer, I went into the alley and opened the city's manhole. Low and behold, the city sewer was plugged, which meant many other homes on that street were also backed up and flooding with sewage. I called the city again.

"We have a problem," I said. "I called you earlier. Your guy said the sewer was open. It is not open. Now I am at a home that has sewage flooding the basement."

Within the hour, a city crew arrived. They pulled off the manhole cover and hooked up a jetter, which shoots out water with enough pressure to clear any blockage in its path. It worked. They cleared the obstruction and opened the sewer.

I went back into the house, down the basement stairs, and watched the sewage drain out faster than it had come in. The smell lingered in the room and my nose. I could not escape it. I told the city crew their sewer backup caused my customer's basement to flood with sewage.

They responded in a way I did not expect. Three city workers went down to the basement and cleaned everything. They moved the books and furniture, sanitized everything, and did not charge the homeowners a dime. They even paid my bill.

Now that is a well-run city.

SO FRESH AND SO GREEN GREEN!

I have seen all kinds of stuff in rental properties. It is amazing what people leave laying around, even when they know I am coming into their home. One time I received a call from the landlord of a rental building about a broken water heater in one of the units. He warned the tenants I was coming. The building had two businesses on the first floor and two units on the second floor. I knocked on unit B's door. No one answered. I knocked a few more times and still no answer. I had the keys to all my rental units. I pulled out unit B's and let myself inside. The place looked empty. A few pieces of clothing were scattered on the living room carpet. A couple dirty dishes sat on the kitchen counter. I walked back to the bedroom that had the broken water heater. The door was closed.

"Hello? Is anyone there? I am Andy, the plumber," I said, lightly knocking on the door.

Even though I suspected no one was home, I wanted to double-check, just to make sure. I knocked a couple more times. No one responded. I went inside. It was a large room, about twenty-five feet long and fifteen feet wide. Stuff was scattered here and there, a typical mess for a college student. The bed blocked the water heater, so I had to move it. I stood up the mattress and looked down.

"What the heck is that?" I said to myself, unable to decipher what was inside a large, semi-clear, plastic bag laying on the bedframe.

I looked closer, and then it became clear – at least a pound of marijuana along with thousands of dollars. One hundred dollar and twenty-dollar bills spilled out from the top of the bag.

"Who would leave their drugs and drug money in such a visible place when they know a plumber is coming to fix the water heater behind the bed?" I thought.

Knowing fully well to not leave my fingerprints on the stuff, I put on gloves, carefully picked up the bag and moved it to the side. I then removed my gloves, finished moving the bed and repaired the water heater. The job took about ten minutes. Before moving the cash and drugs back to the exact spot where I found them, I put my gloves back on. I then laid down the mattress and left. Lucky for that tenant I was not a plumber by day and cop by night.

That day was not the only time I discovered drugs on a job. Many months later, another landlord called me to fix a bedroom heater in one of his rental homes. The house was two stories with five bedrooms, three on the main floor, two on the second floor. I had worked on various jobs at the house during the past seventeen years, so I knew it well. Out of courtesy, I knocked on the door, even though the landlord told the tenants I was coming. No one answered. I let myself inside, checked the faucets and pipes to make sure they were working properly and made my way to the bedroom. The room was chilly and a mess. Clothes and magazines covered the floor. Light shined through the louvered closet door.

"Why is the closet light on?" I thought.

As the saying goes, curiosity killed the cat. I opened the door. A five-foot-tall marijuana plant stood in the middle of the closet. The grow light hovered over it. If I had been a narc, that tenant would have been in serious trouble. Lucky for him, I was the plumber. I cautiously closed the closet door, making sure to not touch anything inside. I then fixed the heater and left.

MY MAGIC CARPET RIDE

On a late Monday afternoon, I received another call from the same house where I found the dildo and fake vagina.

The call came in many years after that incident. A management company had bought the property and made the tenants move out so it could do a thorough clean-out, which included fixing almost everything. The company called me because it needed valves shut off. When I arrived at the property, a woman who worked for the management company greeted me.

"Did you bring bug spray?" she asked.

"Bug spray?" I replied, surprised by the question. "What do you mean?"

"Here," she said, tossing me a can of bug spray. "Take mine. Spray your boots and pants. We need to get in and out as fast as we can."

"Okay," I said, grateful she was looking out for me.

We went inside and walked to unit 2's door on the main floor.

"Here is the deal," she explained. "This place had animals."

Without providing any more information, she opened the door. I followed her through the kitchen, living room, and into the dining room. The dark brown, hardwood floor was moving like a wave of water.

"What is that?" I said, pointing to the moving floor.

It was the first time I had ever seen a hardwood floor move that way. It looked like a magic carpet, swaying slowly back and forth.

"Those are fleas," she stated.

I followed her to another room. It had beige carpeting, which was covered with little, brown, hard-backed fleas. Imagine a million fleas in a five-foot area. They were everywhere.

"We have spray bombed this once already," explained the woman. "It did not affect them."

Shaking my head, I walked out and headed into the bathroom. I could not believe people had been living among that sea of fleas. It was disgusting.

In the bathroom, I shut off a couple valves, which was the only task they wanted me to do that day. I then walked back through the flea-infested rooms and left. The woman followed.

Standing in the driveway, I looked down at my legs. Fleas clung to them.

"This is horrible!" I exclaimed.

"I know," said the woman.

I retrieved my short-handled broom from the back of my truck and smacked the critters repeatedly. I then swept them off my boots and socks. I did not want to take any of them home with me. The woman was wearing shorts. Fleas covered her bare skin. I helped her sweep them off, and we left.

I never went back to that house. A flea infestation is where I draw the line.

WHO LET THE CATS OUT?

On a cold, winter day, I received a call. Two women, both in their sixties, needed the gas line replaced under their kitchen sink. I knew the women well. They worked at a veterinary clinic and loved cats. I assumed they owned a few cats, maybe four or five. I learned later I was wrong.

The women lived in a ranch-style home surrounded by woods. When one of them opened the door to greet me, the smell of urine wafted out.

"Oh no," I thought. "This is not a good sign."

"We need the gas line replaced," explained the woman. "It goes to my cooktop."

She then said the usual line I hear from almost every customer, "Oh, I am going to clean up my house. I have been meaning to do that," which I always assume is a bald-faced lie.

"I am sorry about the cats," she said, as I walked inside. "You know we love cats."

"Yes, I know," I replied.

The house was a million times worse than I had expected. My nose burned from the pungent smell of ammonia. I could not escape it. Cats were everywhere - on the counter, table, shelves, and furniture. In every space a cat could go, there was one. Cat hair was everywhere too. A thick layer covered the floor. At least twenty-five litter boxes were scattered throughout the house, which the cats missed often. Nuggets of poop and urine stuck to the floor.

I kneeled on the stained, hair-covered kitchen floor to look underneath the stove, which was against the wall and self-contained. The cooktop was on the counter with a cabinet underneath. When I opened the cabinet door, a waft of ammonia blew into my face. It looked and smelled like the entire cabinet was covered in urine. With cats watching my every move, I searched for the gas line. When I found it, I could not believe what I saw.

"What is that?" I said to myself (and the cats). The women were in another room.

The cats had peed on the steel line so many times, it had rusted into two. The steel was rotting away, stained with dried urine. I took out my wrenches, removed the line, and installed a new iron pipe. While it was not a difficult job, it was a nasty one. The women had mentioned they were getting a new cooktop and I could see why. The whole thing was rusted out.

A couple months after that job, the women called me again. They needed the ductwork replaced in a few rooms. I agreed to do the work, this time, knowing what was ahead of me.

"I cleaned up a bit because I knew you were coming," said one of the women as she answered the door.

"Yeah, right," I thought. "You should have burned down the place. That would have been better."

I went into the basement. It was Groundhog Day all over again. Cat pee and poop were everywhere. The ammonia smell permeated the air, clinging to my nose. Since the ductwork was above the ceiling, I had to take down a part of it to access the pipes. Using a saw, I cut out the part I needed and looked up at the pipes. Daylight was shining through them. Ductwork pipes are made of sheet metal. You are not supposed to see through them. Those pipes were so rusty, I could see the sunlight through them. The cats had peed on the walls and floors so many times, the urine had seeped down, rusting out the pipes. I went upstairs to find the registers, which are from where the air comes out. All four registers were balls of solid rust. Air was blowing down into the basement, missing the main rooms because the registers had holes in them. I had to replace ten feet of pipe on each register. That is forty feet of rusted sheet metal.

Because I wanted to get the job done quickly, I brought two assistants with me. The guys were so disgusted they almost quit. One of them, who was a meticulously clean person, complained the entire time.

"This is ridiculous!" he whined.

"I am sorry you have to do this," I explained. "But they are not going to change their ways."

The guys gagged as they worked.

"I am burning these clothes tonight," one said.

When we were finished, I smashed the sheet metal and threw it away. Everything stunk.

The women called me a few years later. The ductwork needed replacing again. I went back with an assistant, quickly replaced it and ran out of there. That time I installed plastic registers, which were unaffected by cat urine.

I found out later that sixty-five cats lived in that house. How can anyone live with sixty-five cats? While I do not mind cats, I am more of a dog person. Although even if I loved dogs more than anything in the world, I would never own sixty-five of them.

Looking back, I think that initial call for the gas line replacement was to prepare me for the ductwork. They needed me to get my feet wet….with cat urine.

PRACTICE DOESN'T ALWAYS MAKE PERFECT

With more than thirty years of plumbing under my belt, I am good at what I do. I love the jobs where I show up, and the customer says, "We had another plumber here, and he did not know what to do."

Fueled with motivation, I decide right then and there I will not stop until I find the solution, which I always do. Sometimes, however, the jobs take unexpected twists and turns before I cross the finish line. And no matter how unpredictable a job may be, the customer must pay me for the time, even if a what-would-have-been-two-hour job takes two days.

One warm, summer day, I went on one of those twisty turning jobs. An older fellow called me about a plugged sewer. He owned a large, two-story home, which was all brick and had a pool. The sewer was in a narrow alley that butted up against the back of the home.

When I arrived, the fellow came outside to greet me.

"The sewer is plugged," he said. "Not sure why."

"Okay," I replied. "May I go inside your home first to check out some things?"

I always prefer to look inside a home first before heading to the sewer. It is a good starting point for identifying the problem. I flushed the toilet to confirm it was plugged. We then went back outside to find the cleanout, which is where I could access the sewer from above ground. I pulled off the cap. Considering it did not have any sewage in it, I knew whatever was obstructing the sewer was located closer to the house. If it were farther, I would have seen sewage in the cap.

I retrieved my sewer machine and dropped the cable down, directing it closer to the house. I hit obstructions and kept working at it, pushing the cable through each one. I thought I had fixed the problem; however, the sewer was still plugged. I shoved more cable down, yet the sewer remained plugged.

"This is getting ridiculous," I muttered to myself, a bit concerned I was not making any progress.

Since the cable was underground, I had little visibility into what it was hitting and where it was going. Suddenly, I heard barking. It was a low, deep bark, coming from what seemed like a large dog. The fellow, however, did not own a dog. Puzzled, I peeked into the neighbor's yard. Sure enough, there was a dog pen, and a dog, which looked like a Pit Bull Terrier. The dog was excitedly circling a black cable, which flopped wildly on the ground. Every time the cable moved, the dog barked, jumping from side to side.

"What the hell?" I said.

The fellow was standing next to me.

"What is that?" he asked.

I looked closer. It was my sewer machine cable. I had shoved it so far into the ground that eight feet of it had resurfaced directly in the middle of the dog pen. The dog continued barking and biting at it. I shoved the cable down a little further just to tease him a bit. The fellow and I could not stop laughing.

While that moment was hilarious, the aftermath was not. I used my excavator to dig up the ground and see where I broke through. It turned out I went the wrong way with my sewer machine, breaking through the Y fitting, which is a Y-shaped part underground that connects to multiple sewer lines. I removed the fitting and repaired the sewer pipe, which took a day. I then moved my sewer machine closer to the house, and cut through a bunch of tree roots, finally unplugging the sewer.

The job should have taken one hour and cost one hundred sixty dollars. Because of my mistake, however, it took seven hours and cost eight hundred dollars. Luckily, the fellow paid the bill without any pushback. He understood. Sometimes there are situations plumbers cannot control. I cannot guarantee the job will go smoothly because I never know what I am going to find. I have broken tile with my sewer machine, which cost the homeowner two thousand dollars to fix. If the tile is old, it collapses. It happens, and there is nothing I can do about it.

While most customers understand the charges, some do not. One time, I had to dig up a sewer that served twelve homes. Nobody owned the sewer, which was unusual. I received the call because sewage was spilling into a woman's crawl space. I went to her home to assess the situation.

"I can go into your yard and install two cleanouts," I said.

"Okay, please do it. Do whatever it takes to fix the problem," she responded.

I dug in two cleanouts, removed roots that were blocking the line, and confirmed everything was working.

A couple days later, she called me back.

"The sewer is plugged again," she said. "Can you come back?"

I went back and noticed other residents were having problems too. I interviewed them to get more information and talked to the city. I stopped in one of the neighbor's yards. The house was the furthest downstream, close to the city's mainline. Using my excavator, I dug out the sewer in the neighbor's yard. Nothing came out, which was strange considering all the other homes' sewage flowed down that same pipe. The line should have been filled with sewage. I cut the pipe, installed a cleanout, and reconnected everything.

Knowing the obstruction was further upstream, I set up my sewer machine and pushed the cable into the line. About seventy feet upstream, I hit something. I kept working on it until finally breaking through. The sewage rapidly flowed through the pipe. I never found out what caused the blockage, although I assumed it was tree roots.

The entire project cost sixteen hundred dollars. Because it was a shared sewer, I billed the twelve homeowners two hundred fifty dollars each. Everyone paid without complaining except for one lady. She wrote me a note.

"I will pay this, but it is under protest," it said.

She had sewage spilling into yard yet did not want to pay when I fixed the problem. Little did she know, that bill was nothing compared to another job I accidentally botched.

It was springtime. A homeowner called saying he had water issues in the basement. I had worked on projects at the house before, so I knew the owners well. They were an older couple. The husband was usually the one who called me but ten seconds into our conversation, the wife would take over. That day she was all nerved up.

"We have a continuous problem in our basement," she said. "Every time it rains, the basement floods with water and sewage. Can you please come fix it? It is horrible!"

I could not blame her for being frazzled. In her town, the sewer and surface water drainage are tied together. When it rains significantly, it causes flooding, leaving basements like hers covered with watered down sewage.

"There are two things we can do," I explained. "First, we can break the concrete floor and install a backwater valve, forcing the sewage and water to flow out of the house. Or, we could do replumbing in the basement."

"Do whatever you think is best," she replied.

I like when customers let me make the decision because it gives me the freedom to change the plan as I go. If customers specify they want one course of action, such as installing a backwater valve, and I do not end up installing it due to an unexpected issue, it is difficult to convince them I changed course for their benefit. In plumbing, sometimes you must make things up as you go. It depends what you find along the way.

I chose to break the concrete. I did not like burying a backwater valve under the floor, so I found a way to put a small one above the concrete. That way it would be more accessible if something gets stuck inside.

When my assistant and I arrived, the wife greeted us. She was a middle-aged lady with short, brownish-gray hair. She wore reading glasses that had red rims and a chain.

"Hello," she said. "Follow me to the basement."

We went downstairs. The concrete floor was smashed. Large spider cracks spread across it. A small room, which was hard to access, was to the right of the stairs. The main room contained the washer, dryer, furnace, and water heater. There was another room without a door. It contained yard furniture, which was rotted from water damage. The whole basement smelled like mildew, not sewage. The floor was not flooded, although it was damp.

We walked over to the washer and dryer. The concrete was so cracked and lousy, we could pop it right out. We used our rotary hammer to break it up more. We threw the concrete into buckets, hauled it upstairs and dumped it in our truck. My assistant was half my age, so he did most of the lugging. It would have killed me to do it all. Once the concrete was dug out, I took a step back and thought about how I would have engineered the plumbing differently. Someone else had installed it and did not do a good job.

My assistant and I ran piping above the floor and around the wall. We installed fittings and the backwater valve above the floor. I also installed a cleanout above the concrete, giving me easy access to the sewer in case it plugged. It would have cost the homeowners a lot more money anyway to put it outside – money that most people do not want to spend. I began putting everything back together underneath the floor.

The entire job was going to take at least a couple days, so once we poured the concrete, we called it a night. I took off the cap for the cleanout and stuck it over a fitting.

"We will be back," I told the owners and left.

Around 6 p.m. that evening, a heavy rain showered the town. Two hours later, the wife called. She was hysterical.

"Sewage is coming into the basement!" she yelled. "I do not know what is going on! You must come back now!"

I was surprised and confused.

"How could that be?" I asked. "We fixed the piping and installed the backwater valve."

I thought back on every step I took that day, and then it hit me.

"Oh crap," I thought. "I do not think I glued on the cleanout cap."

I rushed over to her house wearing my hip waders. The wife answered the door. She was so nerved out she was vibrating.

"There is a brand-new furnace down there!" she exclaimed. "I do not know why this is happening!"

"Hang on," I said. "Let me look."

I walked down the basement stairs. Sure enough, a foot of watered-down sewage covered the floor. It smelled like crap too, obviously. Clumps of toilet paper, poop and tampons stuck out of the water. I looked at the furnace. The sewage flooded it too, and the washer and dryer.

"Awe, man," I said to myself.

I waded through the shit swamp, clutching my pump. Near the cleanout, I hooked up the hose and began pumping down the water. I spotted the cleanout cap floating around the sewage. With gloves on, I grabbed the cap and shoved it back onto the cleanout.

Finally, the rain stopped. I pulled the cap off slightly to check it. The sewage was flowing in the opposite direction away from the house. I grabbed a hose, washed down the whole place and made sure to glue down the cleanout cap. Once everything was clean and working as it should, I walked over to the furnace. I remembered installing it just a year ago. Sadly, the sewage had ruined it. I ordered another one, on my own dime, of course.

I walked over to the washer and dryer. They were also destroyed.

"I am so stupid," I muttered to myself. "I should have glued on that cap."

Now I was nerved up. All I wanted to do was get things cleaned up and make it right. I did not tell the owners the mess was my fault. If customers know something like that, they may make you replace everything in the house claiming it was your fault. I replaced everything I broke and did not charge the owners a dime for any of it. They did not ask questions either. If they had, I would have told them about my mistake.

"I fixed the problem, and also replaced your furnace," I told the wife. "I am happy to replace your washer and dryer as well. I will pay for it."

"Do not worry about it," she said. "Those were old anyway."

I nearly hugged her for saying that. A new washer and dryer would have cost me another thousand dollars or more.

Once we all calmed down, I removed a pile of stuff from the basement and made sure everything was sparkling clean. I did not leave until 10 p.m.

That job was supposed to take one day and would have cost around one thousand dollars. Because of my mistake, however, it took five hours longer, and I lost four hundred dollars due to the furnace replacement.

It all worked out in the end, though. The owners were so grateful I had permanently fixed everything, they continued calling me for work years down the road.

The handful of times I have made mistakes, the jobs usually had a happy ending. I solved the problem, and the customers were happy. Only one time was I taken to the cleaners. It was for a four thousand six-hundred-dollar job. I installed a boiler on a dairy farm, and it worked perfectly. I had heard the owner was shady but ignored the claims. I sent him the bill multiple times, which he refused to pay.

"This boiler is not doing what it is supposed to do," he said, coldly. "I am having someone else come and install two water heaters instead. Take your stuff out."

He was a jerk. I went to the farm to remove my equipment. When I arrived, I noticed the pumps I had purchased and installed did not have water running through them. The water lubricates the pumps so if water does not continuously flow through them, they dry out.

"You broke my pumps," I said to the owner. "Those were brand new. You owe me three hundred dollars."

A couple days later, he stopped by my shop with a three-hundred-dollar check in-hand.

"This is all you are getting," he said. "And I want to keep both those pumps."

The second after I gave him the pumps, he darted outside and jumped in his car. I knew he was headed straight to the bank to stop the check before I deposited it.

I ran to my truck and sped to the same bank. Fortunately, I arrived first and deposited his $300 check for a more than four-thousand-dollar job. Never again had I dealt with anyone who was so dishonest.

DETECTIVE DIRTY WORK

Only one time during my plumbing career have I felt in danger. A bank asked me to winterize a home. The bank had tried many times to contact the owner because he was not paying his bills. After four months without any payments, the bank decided to repossess the house. To this day, I suspect the bank wanted me to do its dirty work. The bank knew shenanigans were going on inside the home but did not want to get involved. So, it hired a plumber – me – to "winterize" the house. I knew what the bank really wanted, however, was for me to check out the place.

I felt a bit uneasy that the bank had no idea if the homeowner was still living in the home or had moved elsewhere; however the job seemed interesting. Of course, I did not tell my wife about it. There was no need to make her worry.

My assistant and I pulled up to the house on a sunny, fall afternoon. We were not scared, just cautious. I had driven by the place many times, so I was familiar with the layout. A car and truck were parked in the gravel driveway. The house needed a new coat of paint and a new roof. It had changed hands a couple times. No one did a good job taking care of it. A garage and large, rundown barn were in the backyard.

We knocked on the front door a couple times. No one answered. I slipped the bank's key in the keyhole and slowly opened the door. My assistant and I decided to stick together the entire time, to be extra careful. We did not carry weapons with us. I had a knife and club in my truck, which I had never used.

Inside the place, junk was scattered everywhere. It looked like a bachelor's pad. Pots and pans piled up in the sink and on the stove. Clothing covered the floor. We spotted an old, wooden cabinet in the living room. We jiggled the doors. It was locked. Curious about what was inside, we looked for the key. In a glass bowl near the front door, we spotted a key ring that held dozens of keys. We slipped each one into the keyhole until the cabinet unlocked. A large weapon collection stared us in the face. There were several hundred rounds of ammo and at least four pistols, one of which was a six-shooter. There were also a few semi-automatics, one high powered rifle, and three shotguns. Other paraphernalia, including large knives, sat next to the guns. Near the cabinet, we saw another rifle laying on a coffee table.

We could not believe the owner would leave behind his weaponry, paraphernalia, clothing, furniture, dishes, and other belongings. It looked like he hurriedly fled, most likely knowing he was being chased by the bank or police.

"Holy shit," I thought. "What if this guy comes back and finds us here?"

Slightly more nervous, I kept looking over my shoulder, glancing outside the windows and listening for sounds of someone coming home. If we heard anything, we planned to get the hell out of there. I assumed the owner was not smart enough to have installed cameras, although I did look for them.

Snapping out of detective dirty-work mode, my assistant and I got to work. We put antifreeze in the traps, toilet and kitchen drain, and winterized the water softener. We went down into the basement, which was trashed. Junky furniture, papers, cans, and other garbage littered the floor. We stumbled through the junk without flashlights. I kept looking over my shoulder, expecting to see the owner show up any minute, or a more gruesome thought - hanging from a rafter.

We winterized the well-pump and went back outside to assess the exterior buildings. In the garage, there was an old pickup truck, half of which was taken apart. Tools were scattered around it as if someone was in the middle of fixing the truck but had to flee quickly. In the barn, there were tractors and wagons that looked like they had not been touched in years. Layers of dirt covered every inch of them.

After finishing the job, we went back to the shop, still in disbelief of the arsenal we found and overall mysteriousness of the experience. The bank asked me a slew of follow-up questions. It wanted more information about the condition of the house and what was in it. I reported everything. That night, I told my wife about the job. She rolled her eyes, displeased.

I never found out what happened to the homeowner or his collection of weapons. I assumed the bank repossessed the house and heard the police arrested the owner.

A MOMENT OF REFLECTION

I always liked helping people, which is one reason I became a plumber. I also like taking on jobs other people cannot do. When I figure out the solution, I love seeing people's reaction. Many times, they cannot believe I solved the problem.

From time to time, people have been displeased with me. Some even used the "F" word, pushing their nose against mine like they wanted to fight. Most of the time, I stood there and took it knowing I could charge them extra for being an ass. Most people, however, are so nice I wish I could do the job for free. Those are the customers that become friends. They are always appreciative, which makes me feel good.

I am well respected in my community, especially since I am one of few plumbers in the area. People typically cannot do what I do or do not want to do it. When I am cleaning a sewer or wading through crap, I think to myself, "Not many people would do this." They do not know what to do or how to do it. I have worked for highly educated people who do not understand what I do.

Plumbing is an essential trade. Someone must do it, and I am proud that person is me. Plumbers make good money, too. My wife and I started with nothing. We have done so well during the years; I could retire today. Although I like to work. I will probably retire when I am in my sixties or when my body can no longer take it. At that point, I would rather spend the money we saved and have fun.

CHAPTER 8
CRAIG

When I was 19 years old, my dad got sick. I had graduated high school and was about to go to college. Three months later, we lost him. He did not have life insurance, and my mom had a mortgage to pay. Refusing to leave her under those conditions, I chose to go to work instead of college.

I started driving a truck. My dad was a truck driver. I figured it was best to follow in his footsteps. A few months in the job, however, one of my dad's friends approached me about plumbing.

"Listen," he said. "Your dad would not want you to be a truck driver. How about being a plumber?"

The guy's son had married a plumbing contractor's daughter. He said the contractor would be happy to hire me. While I did not know anything about plumbing, I enjoyed working with my hands. God also graced me with mechanical abilities. Combine those two skills, and anyone could see plumbing would be a natural fit.

I started my career working for a plumbing company that worked on residential homes and mid-rises. I then moved to another company, where I focused on multi-residential condominium and commercial buildings. More than two decades later, I bought that company.

When I look back at my more than fifty years of plumbing, I feel grateful. I rose the ranks quickly moving from apprentice to journeyman to foreman to general superintendent to co-owner. I was elected President of the Plumbing Contractors Association and appointed to represent the West Side Contractors Association as a trustee on the UA Local 130.

Now, at 71-years-old, I am happily retired.

I am Craig, and these are my diaries.

THE EXHIBITIONIST

I admit some plumbers are assholes when it comes to women. Although some women are exhibitionists. I have seen a few "shows" while on jobs, and believe me, the women knew we were watching.

One time, I was called to work on a new construction building in the northern suburbs of Chicago. The buildings were a "four plus one," meaning the ground level was for parking, and the four levels above were residential apartments. An existing building stood next to the new construction site. It was filled with residents, including one woman who I will never forget.

Every morning, all the trade workers assigned to the building – the electricians, carpenters, and plumbers – received a showstopper "welcome to work." A woman who lived in the building next to our site would leave the drapes open while she got dressed in the morning. She was nice looking, probably in her late twenties with shoulder-length red hair. We watched, standing there frozen with our eyes wide open, as she slowly peeled off her pajamas and slipped on her clothes.

We took turns watching her, and she knew it. She wanted to put on a show. Every now and then, she would glance up at us as we stared directly at her. She did not shut the drapes nor turn around. She just kept going, slowly removing one piece of clothing at a time.

"Boy, does she have a beautiful rack!" shouted one of the guys.

"Look at that ass!" yelled another.

The show went on for twenty minutes every morning. Eventually, the bricklayers began putting up walls, one of which blocked our view. While the mortar was still soft, the guys knocked out the bricks, doing whatever it took to not miss the show. It certainly made my job more exciting.

That woman was not the only exhibitionist. One time I was working on a high rise, new construction building. We were using a transit level, which is essentially a telescope on a tripod. It magnifies everything. We stood up the transit level to look inside the surrounding buildings. A handful of airline stewardesses lived in one of them. They got dressed every morning with the drapes wide open. For a month, we watched the ladies slip on their uniforms.

Why didn't they close the drapes?

On another call, we did not see a naked woman in action per se; however we did see something close to it. Fifty years ago, in housing projects, there was usually a construction office on site, which had a board with slots assigned to each subcontractor. Service calls were written down on papers and shoved into the slots. The foreman went to the office every morning to collect a handful of papers. One of them said a faucet was leaking in the master bathroom of a house. The foreman asked me to assist him on the job.

The home was two stories and made of brick with some siding. We knocked on the door. A woman answered. She was about five-feet, six-inches tall with short, dark hair, and looked to be in her late twenties. She wore beige slacks and a blue short-sleeved shirt, nothing unusual.

"Good morning," I said. "We are here to repair the leak in the master bathroom faucet."

"I am sure you know where the bathroom is," she replied. "Go ahead."

I had worked on several of those homes before, so I knew them well. We walked back to the bathroom to assess the lavatory faucet. I was standing at the sink, operating the hot and cold-water handles when the foreman looked down at the wastebasket.

"Meet me in the truck," he said suddenly, grabbing something out of the wastebasket and running out of the bathroom.

He took off, leaving me alone to fix the faucet. I was curious about why he had bolted; however I knew I had to stay and finish the job. Ten minutes later, I went back downstairs.

"The problem is resolved," I told the woman. "If there are any future problems, let the service department know."

I darted out to the truck. Once we were both inside, the foreman pulled out a Polaroid picture. I could not believe what I saw. The lady was posing on her bed, laying on her side, completely naked. It looked like she was modeling for a Playboy shoot. The foreman was laughing. I was in disbelief. It was not a picture worth dwelling on, so we did not stare at it for too long. Although we did take it with us, and maybe passed it around to other plumbers on the project.

THE BOWL PACKERS

When a toilet is plugged, it is usually because someone put something down the bowl that is not supposed to go down there. Of course, whenever I ask customers if they have flushed anything besides toilet paper, the answer is always "no."

One time, after a husband gave me that response, I used my rodder and pulled out a tampon.

"Sir, this is what was plugging your toilet, and you will receive a bill," I said.

"That is not the brand my wife uses," replied the guy.

How would he know that? The thing was soaked in water.

Another time, I was rodding a toilet for a middle-aged, well-to-do couple in the suburbs. To my surprise, I pulled out a toothbrush.

"Have you been brushing your teeth in the toilet again?" the husband asked his wife.

I thought that was funny.

Another time, when a lady was standing next to me as I rodded her toilet, I pulled out a cotton ball.

"Ma'am, you should not throw cotton balls down the toilet," I said.

"Well, geez, what is the toilet for?" she replied.

Then I pulled out a Q-tip.

"Ma'am, you should not throw Q-tips down the toilet," I said.

"Well, geez, what is the toilet for?" she repeated.

"A toilet is for piss, shit, and toilet paper," I replied bluntly.

She was quiet after that remark.

One time, however, it was not Q-tips, cotton balls, tampons or toothbrushes plugging the toilet. It was just plain old, packed, hard shit.

Many years ago, a friend called me.

"A buddy of mine has a toilet that needs replacing," he said. "It is by your house."

"I will do it," I said.

I arrived at the house in the early evening. It was a ranch-style home, about one thousand square feet, and made of brick. I knocked on the door. The husband answered. He looked to be in his early thirties, about six-foot-tall and had short brown hair.

"I am here to replace your toilet," I said.

"Follow me," he said, opening the door for me to go inside.

The house had three bedrooms, a kitchen, and one bathroom, which was in the center of everything. The room smelled like shit, which, while memorable, did not bother me. To a normal, non-plumber, it would have been unbearable. I, on the other hand, was accustomed to that smell. Their shit was my bread and butter.

I expected the toilet to have a minor problem. When I opened the lid, however, it quickly became clear I was wrong.

"Wow," I thought to myself.

The husband stood next to me, flushed with embarrassment. Not wanting to make things worse for him, I kept my mouth shut.

The Cerulean, blue toilet was filled to the brim with brown poop. It looked like a heavy mud, packed densely in the bowl. Some people poop three times a day; others poop every three days. I did not know this couple's pooping schedule, although I assumed the toilet had been broken for at least a couple days. And again, it was the only toilet in the house.

The aroma was pungent, although it still did not bother me.

"Do you have an empty soup can and a bucket?" I asked the husband.

"Okay," he said.

His face turned a brighter shade of red as he walked out of the room. A couple minutes later, he returned with both items, handed them to me and left. I imagined him cowering in the corner with embarrassment.

I could not remove the toilet without first removing the poop. Using my Channellock, I grabbed the rim of the top of the open can, dropped it into the bowl, scooped out the poop, and dumped it into the bucket. I repeated that motion at least twenty times. While it was the most disgusting thing I had ever done, I forced myself to remain composed. My stomach was not turning, and I had a very strong mind.

"How could people be so stupid to continue filling a toilet that does not work?" I thought.

It took me ten minutes to scoop out all the poop. I then removed the toilet bowl, left it in the backyard, and installed a new one.

"Here is your new toilet," I said to the husband. "Good luck."

"I am so happy I could shit," he replied (just kidding!)

He thanked me, and I left. I charged him slightly more money for that kind of manual labor.

THE OLD MAN AND THE COCKROACHES

In the early eighties, two, four and six flat subsidized housing buildings were scattered across the city. I worked on many of them, one of which I will never forget.

On a crisp, fall day, a general contractor called us. A unit in a four flat building had a broken toilet. Since my partner and I finished another job earlier than expected that day, we had time to fill.

"Sure, we will go there now," I told the contractor.

We pulled up to the building. It was made of brick with two units on each side. Mailboxes with unit numbers and buzzers covered the exterior entry wall. I rang the bell to the unit.

"Yeah?" echoed a man's voice over the intercom.

"We are here to fix the toilet," I said.

"Come in," he said.

The door buzzed. We walked into the building and knocked on the unit's door. A man answered, wearing full-body, white, long underwear that had a flap over his butt. He looked like he was in his sixties, with a slim build and straggly hair. He spoke with a slight southern drawl.

"Go ahead," he said, opening the door wider.

We headed to the bathroom. We knew where it was located because we had worked in similar units many times before. The man sat down at the kitchen table, lit a cigarette, sipped coffee, and ignored us.

We walked past the living and dining rooms on the left, two bedrooms on the right, and into the bathroom. The house was messy. Clothes were scattered across the floor. Dishes were piled high in the kitchen sink. The bathroom was dirty. The once-white vinyl tile was a shade darker. A brown water ring stained the bottom of the tub. The porcelain wall-hung lavatory was dull. The toilet looked like it had never been cleaned. The building was only six months old. It was hard to believe so much dirt had accumulated in such a short period of time.

I began adjusting the legs on the wall-hung lavatory while my partner proceeded to assess the toilet. Sure enough, it was loose. If someone sat down, it rocked back and forth. We needed to remove and reinstall the whole thing. We shut off the water, and my partner got to work. He kneeled, loosened the bolts, and started lifting the toilet off the ground.

"Look at this!" he shouted.

At least thirty cockroaches scurried out from under the toilet. They were an inch-long, had legs on both sides, and black backs. I hurriedly tucked my pant legs into my socks as the cockroaches raced around my boots. While I had not seen that many roaches on a job before, I was not surprised. Most of those units probably had cockroaches. If one was clean, chances are the other three were not. The tenants could not escape them.

My partner set down the toilet and grabbed his hammer.

"Bang!"

He smashed the cockroaches one-by-one like he was playing a game of Whac-A-Mole. Fortunately, the Vinyl floor tiles were the cheapest you could buy. They were soft, twelve-inch squares. A hammer would not cause any damage.

Some of the cockroaches escaped, running into the hallway. We reset the toilet.

"All done!" we told the owner.

"Okay, thanks," he replied, not moving from the kitchen table.

We did not tell him about the cockroaches. Who knows? They may have been his pets.

THERE'S SOMETHING STRANGE... IN THIS SOUTHSIDE HOOD... WHO YOU GONNA CALL?

Oftentimes when we worked on piping projects in downtown Chicago, we excavated the ground. One time, buried in the dirt, we found bottles that looked like they were from the 1800s. Another time, I unearthed antique tiles. I kept moving the shovel back and forth, scraping off the dirt. Sure enough, it was a pool. The lettering said, "shallow end."

Chicago's history lives everywhere – in its soil, on signs, and in its architecture. One well-known historical building was the Lexington Hotel. Chicago's infamous mob boss Al Capone used the hotel as his headquarters from the late twenties to early thirties. The building was torn down more than twenty years ago.

In 2007, I landed a six-million-dollar contract to install plumbing in a new, high-rise condominium building that was being built on the Lexington site. An Irishman bought the property. I was thrilled to win the bid. The money was good, and the project would take about two years to complete, keeping my crews plenty busy.

We had thirty plumbers working on the site at one time. We first installed the underground piping. As the building went up, the other trade crews would pour concrete decks to build support for the next floor. We had to install the piping before they poured the concrete or put in a sleeve which created a hole that we could run the piping through once the concrete was poured. We worked eight hours every day, sometimes six days a week. After they put in the drywall and painted, we went back to install the trim plumbing.

In 2009, the building was finished. The Irishman, however, was having financial problems. The economy crashed. Units were not selling. The Irishman stopped paying the security company, so the alarm and phone systems were turned off.

One day, the superintendent called me.

"I think you better come down to the Lexington," he said panicky. "There has been a big problem. The building got flooded out. It looks like a pipe broke or something like that."

The news was disappointing; however, I knew it was not our fault. The water had been turned on for nine months. It was working fine. If the copper joints were bad, when you turned on the water, you would know immediately or within the next week. Damage after nine months of the water working just fine would be highly unusual.

"I will be right over," I told the superintendent.

I jumped into my car and drove to the site. From the outside, the building looked intact. I did not see any damage. The inside, though, was ruined. Water leaked from the mechanical room on the thirtieth floor into the floors below, flooding all the units. The drywall was peeling. Fortunately, we caught the problem before anything could rot. Still, the whole place looked terrible.

I went up to the mechanical room. A dozen trade workers were gathered around, discussing what could have caused the mess. I spotted the fitting that was pulled off the pipe. The fitting itself was intact. It was a good one too – Victaulic with a coupling on it. Someone must have pulled it off, causing the water to flow outwards. We suspected the fitting had been disconnected for four hours. If the alarm system had been turned on, we would have discovered the leak earlier, possibly the moment the fitting was pulled off.

"I would like to know who did this," I said, angrily.

Anytime there is a problem on a job, I am not happy about it, especially when the damage was caused by a seemingly intentional act.

"We do not know," replied one of the tradesmen, shrugging his shoulders.

"A lot of strange things have happened in this building," said the superintendent.

He did not provide any more details, nor did I ask him to explain what he meant by that comment. The whole incident seemed peculiar. Someone with inside knowledge of the site had to have known where the mechanical room was located, go all the way up there to the top floor, and then remove the fitting. I assumed it was an insider, someone with construction knowledge who was working on the job and a had a big vendetta, or....

"I think it is Al Capone's ghost sabotaging the building," I said.

The building was Al Capone's property. The fellow who bought the property was from Ireland. Capone's rival was the North Side Irish Gang. I suspect he would not want an Irishman owning his property.

The superintendent laughed a bit nervously. He admitted it was a good theory.

From that point on, the insurance company took over the project. Construction resumed about six months later. We were not a part of it. To this day, no one figured out who removed the fitting. I stand by my theory, which would make it the first and last time I encountered a ghost on a job site.

A MOMENT OF REFLECTION

After more than five decades working as a plumber, my memory bank is overloaded. While some general contractors were good, logical, and understanding people, others were extremely unethical. They would take advantage of you. When you give them a proposal to install plumbing in a building, for example, they would accept the proposal and then refuse to pay you. When I ran into those unethical contractors, I not only turned down the job but also spread the word among my association.

"Do not work for that guy," I would say loudly. "He won't pay you. He will cheat you."

Most of the time, customers were nice and appreciative. I remember one job I worked on at a house in Glenview, Illinois. A lady needed me to fix her leaky faucet in the kitchen. When I arrived, she answered the door. Another woman and two kids stood behind her. It looked like they were having a playdate.

"I am here to repair the faucet," I said.

"Come on in!" she said, flashing a welcoming smile.

She walked me to the kitchen, and I got to work. The ladies propped open the patio door to get some fresh air. Although they ended up getting more than air. A bird flew into the kitchen.

"Ahhhhhhh! Help us! Help us!" they screamed, ducking and hovering, not knowing what to do.

"Get me a towel," I said, calmly, hoping everyone would simmer down.

Within minutes, I captured the bird, threw it outside, and watched it fly away.

"Thank you! Oh, thank you so much!" exclaimed one of the ladies, looking at me as if I were a superhero. They were very grateful for my swift, heroic action.

Plumbers are not always just plumbers. We are rescuers, concierges, and listeners. We go into people's homes, treat them with respect, answer their questions, and fix their problems. I do not know if all plumbers would have sprung to capture the bird; however I assume many would. When I see two ladies in distress, of course I will help them.

Some of my favorite plumbing days were when I worked on famous people's homes. I installed the plumbing in former Chicago Mayor Richard M. Daley's townhouse. When the superintendent met me, he made it clear the house was "special."

"There is a special person who will be living in this home," he said.

"Who is it?" I asked.

"I cannot tell you," he said smirking.

He seemed proud to know such an important secret.

One way or another we found out it was the former mayor's home. The project involved installing plastic waste pipes, which were extremely noisy. A cast-iron pipe manufacturer offered to donate piping to the former mayor; however he did not accept the gift. He said he wanted the plumbing in his house to be the same as the plumbing in every other townhouse on the block.

A couple months after Mayor Daley and his wife, Maggie, moved into the home, one of the toilets broke. I volunteered to go to the house and fix it.

The house was a four-story walk-up. I climbed the stairs and rang the bell. The superintendent eagerly stood by my side.

Maggie answered the door.

"Good morning, Mrs. Daley," I said. "I am here to fix your toilet."

"Come inside," she replied. "Go ahead. I will be on the couch watching television."

I walked up to the third-floor bathroom. The toilet had a broken ballcock, which was easy to fix. Once I confirmed everything worked properly, I went back downstairs.

"Mrs. Daley, everything is fixed!" I said. "If you have any other problems, please let us know."

Looking back on my career, I do not remember a time when I did not enjoy it, except towards the end. The community of plumbers and contractors was changing. They were younger and less experienced. They looked at a blueprint, insisting we install something a specific way when I knew their way would not work. Instead of sitting down with contractors to discuss business, looking them in the eye, face-to-face to see if they were an ethical person or a snake, they would simply send text messages or emails. When I left messages, they would not call me back. I never knew who I was dealing with, making the job lose its luster. The people who I trusted were retiring. I knew it was my time too.

Plumbing is a rewarding and profitable career. If you enjoy working with your hands, you will enjoy plumbing. It is like building something with an Erector set every day. My grandfather was a plumber. He used to say:

"If things get bad and your furnace breaks, you can always build a fire. If your electricity goes out, you can always light a candle. But you always need clean water to drink and a place to go poop."

And that is why the world will always need plumbers.

CHAPTER 9
MATT

I grew up in a small town located slightly north of Green Bay, Wisconsin. When I was a teenager, my parents split up, and my mom moved to the northwest suburbs of Chicago. My three older siblings followed her. A few years later, I joined them. I was only 19 years old. With no plans to go to college, I needed a job quickly. At first, I worked as a landscaper, which did not bring in enough money. When I was about to call it quits and move back to Wisconsin, one of my buddies told me about a guy who owned a plumbing company. He said the guy needed an apprentice. Some of my landscaping jobs included a little plumbing, mainly sod work and installing sprinkler systems. For the most part, however, plumbing was a new world, which I was willing to try.

I did not have any preconceived notions. After all, I was raised in the country. We were not the cleanest kids. We had a dog and many other animals.

"Do not worry about your hands getting dirty," my father used to say. "You can wash them later." Applying that same principle to plumbing, I did not wear rubber gloves on jobs until at least six or seven years into my career.

One week after meeting with the owner of the plumbing company, I became his new apprentice. We both quickly discovered that I had a lot to learn. Two weeks into the job, I made a major mistake. In the dead of winter, a homeowner called saying his sewer was backed up. Another plumber and I went to his home to fix it. It was an old, two-story brick house. The homeowner, who was in his mid-forties with short, thinning, brown hair, greeted us at the front door.

"Let's go to the basement," he said.

We followed him downstairs and immediately spotted the sewer. We unsuccessfully tried rodding it from inside. The next day, we came back to install a cleanout. The temperature was in the single digits. The whipping wind made it feel ten degrees colder.

The sewer was nine feet underground in his front yard. We installed a camera and a locator. To clear the line, we had to excavate a nearby parkway. We explained our plan to the homeowner, and he gave us the green light to proceed.

We returned the following day. It was the coldest day Chicago had experienced in years. People stopped by to take pictures of us as we excavated the parkway. They could not believe we were working outside. Halfway through the project, while using a backhoe to dig out the sewer, we cut straight through the main water line. The teeth on the backhoe ripped it apart. Water gushed inside our hole and flooded the street. Chunks of concrete rushed with the water as it moved like a river down the road. It was such a mess; city crews came out to help. They did not want to turn off the water because it was so cold. My boss also came to the rescue with pumps in-hand. The water rose so high, the city finally told us to shut it off. We spent the entire next day fixing my screw up, pumping out water until late in the evening.

The homeowner was not happy. He kept asking when we would repair his sewer considering the water main mishap delayed us several days. My boss took over that relationship.

That incident was the biggest mistake I ever made in my plumbing career. I am grateful it happened during the beginning of it. I learned many lessons that day, including how to properly and improperly use my machinery. Fortunately, my boss was a patient man. I ended up working for him for nine years, mainly unclogging sewers and fixing water main breaks.

Seeking a change, I moved to a service company based in Mount Prospect, Illinois. I enjoy the job because I get to help five or six customers a day. I thrive on helping people. It is the main reason why I love plumbing. I am now fourteen years into my plumbing career, and I am good at it.

I am Matt, and these are my diaries.

IT'S RAINING RUBBERS, HALLELUJAH! (NOT REALLY)

In the beginning of my career, about twelve years ago, on a warm summer day, I received a call from a lady about a clogged sewer.

"My sewer is backing up," she said. "I do not know why it is happening. Can you please help?"

"We will be right over," I said.

My partner and I pulled into the driveway. The house was ranch-style with white, vinyl siding. The driveway, which was made of asphalt, had two lanes, giving us plenty of space to park our machines and truck.

We knocked on the door. A woman answered. She looked to be in her mid-forties with middle-length, straight brown hair, and wire-framed glasses. She wore faded jeans and a white t-shirt.

"Hello," she said. A look of relief washed over her face.

My partner spoke broken English, so I did most of the talking.

"Hello," I said. "I am Matt, the plumber. We are here to fix your sewer."

She invited us inside and led us to the bathroom.

"Every time I flush the toilet, the water will not go down," she explained.

A pool of water circled the base of the toilet, indicating her entire line was backed up. We walked around the outside of the house to assess the cleanout.

"Ma'am, we will need to stick a camera down the line to see what is going on," I said and gave her a price.

"That is not a problem," she replied. "Just do it, please."

The sewer was poorly connected to the house. Years ago, builders used a rubber round coupling called a "Fernco" to hold pipes together. It did not hold up well, causing pipes to slip apart, which was the situation at the woman's home. I set up the underground camera to get a closer look.

"You can watch if you want," I told the woman. I always like offering clients the opportunity to see what is inside their sewers.

"That is okay," the woman replied. "It is a warm, beautiful day. I will mosey around outside."

I lowered my camera underground. Within minutes, I found the slipping pipe.

"Come over here and take a look!" I yelled to the woman.

She came over and saw it for herself. She had only lived in the home for a couple years.

"Yet again, things are half-assed in this home," she muttered.

I hear homeowners murmur similar accusations all the time. They always blame the previous homeowners for making cheap purchases.

"We are going to come back tomorrow with our machine to dig up the sewer," I said.

"See you then," she replied.

The next morning, we pulled into the driveway. The woman came outside to greet us as we unloaded our equipment.

"Good morning!" she said, smiling. "Are you ready to get to work?"

"We are all set, ma'am," I said.

We began excavating the ground in the front yard. An open bedroom window was about fifteen feet to our right. The woman was sitting on the bed, talking to us through the open window.

"It is a beautiful day outside," she said, as we were knee-deep in dirt, digging up the ground. "Maybe I will do a little shopping today. There is a great outdoor mall nearby."

Focused on the job, I did not have time to talk. My chatty boss stood by the window to converse back with her.

"Oh yes, I have been to that mall," he said.

I dug the hole while my partner grabbed a probe to locate the sewer. When we reached the pipe, he jumped into the hole to dig around it. I handed him our partner saw so he could chop up the pipe. He cut out a section and began pulling out wads of tree roots. The roots balled up inside the pipe, collecting anything and everything that had flushed down the toilet. The strong sewer odor crept out of the pipe into our noses. It did not bother me. Considering I unplug sewers almost every day, even the smelliest ones do not turn my stomach.

My partner continued pulling tree roots out of the pipe. With one final pull, a ball of something else came out.

"What the...." I said in a question-statement like fashion.

Leaning in for a closer look, I immediately saw what was dangling in front of us. At least eighty to one hundred used condoms were wrapped around the tree roots. They were white with a tinge of brown, which was most likely the remnants of the sewage.

"What are those?" asked the woman, feigning shock.

She knew exactly what they were and why they were stuck in her sewer. People always deny the personal items we find clogging their lines belong to them, even when they are the only ones living in the house. No one else used the woman's sewer line. We all knew exactly to whom they belonged.

I walked away with a shit-eating grin on my face. My boss stood there silently, slowly turning his back towards the bedroom window. We spent several minutes staring at the white elephant, or in that case, snakes in the room.

"Condoms! Anacondas and condoms!" screamed my partner, breaking the awkward silence with a statement that was even more awkward.

He called tree roots, "anacondas," and clearly knew the word "condom." Everyone, including those who speak English as a second language, knows that word.

I paced the lawn, biting my tongue, trying everything not to laugh out loud. We had all seen condoms before, obviously, but this was more like a collection, and the condom enthusiast was sitting twenty feet away from us.

Desperately wanting to leave, we avoided looking at the woman, even through the window, and got back to work. Surprisingly, she still sat there, watching us. She seemed unbothered by our discovery, sticking to her argument that she had no idea how the condoms ended up inside her sewer.

We repaired the sewer line, backfilled the hole, collected our money and left.

Most of the time, when I pull stuff like tampons and diapers out of sewers, I explain to the homeowners why they should not flush those products down the toilet. In this case, however, I had no words. It was too uncomfortable. I just wanted to finish the job and get out of there.

HOARD OF THE FLIES

I rarely feel disgusted. The only time a job made me gag was when my partner and I installed fifteen grease interceptors at a chain of gas stations. The interceptors were metal boxes buried under the floor. Their purpose was to trap the grease flowing through the pipes while allowing the water to drain out and flow through. Each interceptor took an entire day to replace, which were some of the toughest days of my career. Grease smells worse than shit. The gas stations cooked a lot of pizza. We saw slimy remnants of it when we opened the lids. The grease itself looked like human guts, filling all thirty-five-gallon interceptors to the brim. It was obvious the gas station managers never pumped them out or even looked at them in years. The metal was rotting away. We used cups to scoop out the grease, pouring chunks into bags and buckets. I took many breaks, stepping outside for fresh air, trying to prevent myself from vomiting. Every day, I felt sick. The smell burned my nose, making my stomach churn.

That job was by far the most abhorrent one I had worked on yet and still takes the cake for the most repulsive commercial call. On the residential front, one lady's home I will never forget. While I did not gag or step outside, the home was so filthy, the memory is engrained in my brain.

It was a hot, summer day in Glenview, Illinois, which is a beautiful suburb on the northeast side of Chicago. Our company's dispatch received a call. A woman had an unusually expensive water bill and wanted us to check for leaks. Assuming the job would be easy, I volunteered to check it out by myself. My assumption was wrong. While the fix itself was easy, the journey to get there would be my toughest one yet.

Surrounded by medium-sized, unkempt green bushes, the house was white with chipping paint. It looked tired, had two stories and a deck, which jutted out from the side of the house. It looked like no one had taken care of the home for years. I parked my truck on the street and walked up a narrow sidewalk to the front door. My instructions were to walk into the house and yell, "I am the plumber!" Feeling a bit awkward about barging into someone's home, I called the woman ahead of time.

"Hello ma'am, I am the plumber," I said. "I am outside. May I come in?"

"Yes, go ahead," she replied.

I went inside. The smell of cat pee and shit blew up in my face. The cats must have crapped and urinated all over the place for years. I stood in the foyer area. To the right was the kitchen, and to the left was a stairway leading up to the second bathroom and bedrooms. Newspapers and boxes were everywhere. They were piled high almost to the ceiling, one stack butting up against another. The woman was sitting on the couch in the living room, surrounded by more boxes and newspapers. She was an elderly lady. Her hair was white and stringy, hanging heavy alongside her face. It looked like she had not bathed in weeks. She wore a battered, black robe.

"My water bill was strangely high last month," she said, barely glancing my way. "I hear the toilet down here running sometimes. Maybe that is the problem."

It sounded like a toilet flapper problem; however I needed to assess all possibilities just to be sure. My goal was to find the exact problem and solve it that day, preferably within the hour, so that I would never have to return.

"May I look around?" I asked.

"Go ahead," she said, remaining on the couch.

Amidst the endless boxes and newspapers, I followed a skinny path to move from one room to another. The kitchen was by far the grossest. Dirty dishes piled high in both sinks like no one had touched them in months. Moldy, crumbly food was everywhere – on the countertops, round wooden table and on the floor. Swarms of flies buzzed around it. Old pizza boxes were scattered across the floor. Silverware, which was more of a brownish-black color than silver, sat on the counter, table and in the sink. To top everything off, the house was hot. The woman had not turned on the air conditioning, fostering an even cozier environment for the flies. I wanted to get the hell out of there, however knew I had a job to finish first.

I followed the next skinny walkway to the spiraling basement staircase. Surprisingly, the basement was significantly tidier than the rest of the house. A few boxes cluttered the staircase and unfinished floor. I assessed the water heater, looking for signs of a leakage. I did not see any indicators. I went back upstairs, into the sea of papers, boxes and cat pee, and shimmied my way to the staircase that led to the second floor.

Again, surprisingly, the second floor was not that cluttered, although it was filthy. The bathroom looked like it had not been used in years. The bathtub, toilet, and sink were covered in brown stains. The water was shut off. I went back downstairs into the main floor bathroom. Boxes and newspapers filled every nook and cranny of the room. Old, crusty toothbrushes, hairbrushes and empty tubes of toothpaste were scattered around the floor. So much junk cluttered the room, the woman would have to stand sideways against the sink to wash her hands. Two cats raced past the doorway.

"I have to get out of here," I thought, in disgust.

I assessed the flapper, and sure enough, she needed a new one.

"I am headed to my truck!" I yelled as if she even cared. "I will be right back."

The minute I walked outside, I called my service manager.

"This house is bad," I said. "She is a hoarder. It stinks. I hate this."

"Just hurry up and do the repair," he replied.

I grabbed a new flapper and went back inside. It took me a minute to replace it, much shorter than the process of assessing the problem. At least I knew though, I found a permanent fix, which meant I would never have to return. In a hurry to get out of there, I told the woman to only pay me the service fee, which was thirty-nine dollars. She handed me a check, and I left.

On the way home, still feeling disgusted, I thought about how a person could let their home deteriorate to that extent. Then, I felt sorry for her. She most likely had no one around to help her. Her family was her cats. It is sad to think people may be living so alone in this world. I gave my three kids and wife an extra-long hug that night.

A MOMENT OF REFLECTION

Fortunately, I have experienced minimal dramatic moments during my plumbing career. I have never had an angry customer. No one has kicked me out of their home when I told them the cost of my services. I had a couple scares while digging out deep sewers. My old company did not believe in shoring to hold up the walls. They collapsed at times but thank goodness no one was buried under them. We had close calls though. I remember yelling at a guy, "Jump on the ladder as fast as you can!"

For the most part, however, our plumbing calls usually go as planned and are uneventful.

I like being a blue-collar worker. I rarely deal with a boss. I drive around in my truck, doing my own thing, and taking care of customers. It makes me feel good to know I helped get someone's sewer line back on track, preventing sewage from flooding their home, or fixed their water heater so they could take a hot shower. I fix basic services that families need. They need hot water and a working sewer. If either of those services do not work, their world comes crumbling down. People take those luxuries for granted until they break.

Plumbing is a good career. Every plumbing company I know is looking to hire people. It is tough to find good plumbers. When I first started, it was a gamble. I knew very little about the industry. Now I know I made the right move. I enjoyed it the first day as much as I enjoy it today. Every day brings a new experience, whether it is installing or unclogging toilets, repairing sump pumps or water main breaks, or digging out sewers. Every customer has different needs making every day different.

Most people have an image of a plumber as an overweight man, who shows too much crack, dresses shitty, smells and drinks too much beer. That image is an inaccurate stereotype, at least for most of us. Plumbers are like doctors, however, instead of fixing your body, we fix your mechanical systems. We wear uniforms and drive business branded trucks. We value our work and enjoy helping people.

I am happy with the career choice I made and cannot imagine doing anything else.

CHAPTER 10
JAC

When I was a kid, my dad frequently asked me to help him with projects around the house. My small hands changed garbage disposals, fixed toilets, and worked on cars. I had a learning disability, which made school difficult. When I watched someone fix something, however, it felt like my disability had disappeared. I picked it up quickly and felt confident in my newfound skills.

My first real job was working as a bartender. I then became a teamster truck driver. Eleven years later, however, I hurt my back, to the point where I could no longer drive a truck. I was also a recovering alcoholic, which led me to a job working as a drug and alcohol counselor. With a wealth of knowledge (and heart) to pass onto people who were struggling with addictions, that job was my universe. I loved every minute of it.

Sadly, nine years into it, I was diagnosed with an environmental illness. Perfume, cologne, soaps, cleaning products, and many other substances severely disrupted my nervous system, to the point where it could shut down. The doctors said environmental illnesses were caused by stress. Considering my dad was an angry alcoholic (he threw an ashtray that broke my brother's nose when he was just three years old), I had a hunch the stress derived from my childhood.

Because of my illness, I could no longer work in public. I quit being a counselor, which was heartbreaking. My therapist helped a lot during that time.

"What will I do?" I asked her. "I cannot work in public."

I felt lost.

"Jac," she said "In your building, don't you do all the plumbing?"

Two decades ago, I moved into an apartment building in Oakland, California, to be the building's manager. The prior manager was doing a piss-poor job, so the owner moved her out and moved me in. The 32-unit, stucco building was more than a 100 years old.

I loved my fellow tenants and owned a bunch of plumbing tools (after all those years helping my dad fix things, I became quite the handywoman), so whenever problems arose, I came to the rescue. One of my biggest complaints was a sewage leak in the basement. For an entire year I complained to the building owner about sewage dripping onto the basement floor. Finally, a plumber came over to fix it. I walked him down to the basement, showed him the leaking sewage and went back to my apartment. He knocked on my door an hour later.

"I cannot find the leak," he said.

"Alright, let me help," I replied, grabbing my tool bag.

I believed the source of the leak was a pipe in the wall between the third and fourth floor. The wall was made of lath and plaster. To cut through it, we needed a special kind of saw, which the plumber did not own. Luckily for him, I owned one. After sawing through the wall, I used a mirror and a flashlight to look inside. Within minutes I spotted the source - a cast iron pipe that was about four inches long.

While the plumber fixed the leak, we used my strategy and tools to find it. In other words, I did eighty percent of the work. So, when my therapist suggested I should be a plumber, I felt confident in my abilities, although not so much in my business management skills.

"Start my own business?" I asked her, thinking the idea was ludicrous.

"Yes," she replied. "You should start your own plumbing business."

"But I have a learning disability," I said. "I cannot run my own business."

"You will learn," she said.

"I cannot pull a toilet," I said. "I do not know how to do that."

"You will learn," she repeated, confidently. "What plumbing do you do in the building?"

"I fix toilets and clear tub drains," I said. "I do it because I love the tenants."

"You need to get paid for that," she replied. "You get free rent and a few hundred bucks a month. You need to get paid for plumbing too."

With her words stuck inside my head, I stopped by the building owner's office to pick up my management check.

"Hey Joe," I said. "You know that plumber who came by to finally fix the leak?"

"Yes," he muttered, staring at his computer screen.

"How much did you pay him for that job?" I asked.

"Go look at the checks yourself," he said, pointing to a file drawer.

I rifled through the checks until I found the one belonging to the plumber.

"Eight hundred dollars!" I yelled. "I did eighty percent of the work, and he got eight hundred dollars?"

I could not believe it.

"Joe," I said. "From now on, I want to do all the plumbing in the building. You can pay me twenty bucks an hour. If a job is bigger than what I can do, I will let you know."

"Deal," he replied, without hesitation.

From that moment on, I did all the plumbing in the building and started making good money. Wanting to advance my career, I applied for a job at a plumbing company. After the interview, the owner walked me to the door.

"How did you feel about that interview?" he asked.

"I think you love me," I confidently replied. "Your boys, on the other hand, do not feel the same way." His "boys" were the other male plumbers who worked for him.

"I noticed that too," he said. "How can they not have the same feeling as I do?"

"They are threatened," I said.

"Jac," he said. "Can you do shower valves? You know those guys have been working for me for thirty years, and they cannot do shower valves."

"I can do shower valves," I said.

"You are hired," he said, extending his arm for a handshake to seal the deal.

"Great! When should I start?" I replied excitedly.

"Today is Friday. Let's start on Tuesday. Before you come, call me in the morning," he said and walked back to his office.

Feeling proud, I left with a skip in my step. That Tuesday morning was September 11, 2001. When I turned on the television, like most people on that horrific day, tears welled up in my eyes. I called my new boss.

"Are you watching the news?" I asked.

"My gosh, Jac," he said, sounding devastated. "My whole family is in New York. I really want you to work for me, but I might move to New York. I cannot stand staying here, thinking my family is there."

He was understandably rattled.

"I will call you in a few days," he said.

Less than a week later, he sold his plumbing business and moved back to New York. I went back to my therapist, not knowing what to do next.

"Listen," she said. "Go out there and do it on your own."

Feeling motivated, I started placing advertisements everywhere – in physical locations and online. One day, a man named Martin called me.

"Are you hiring plumbers?" he asked.

"Well, I do not have a business right now, although I am building it. How much do you want to be paid?" I asked.

"How about fourteen dollars an hour?" he eagerly replied.

"Okay," I said. "If I get work, I will call you."

One week later, he called again.

"Are you hiring a plumber?" he asked. I appreciated his tenacity.

"I told you if I got a job, I would call you," I gently replied.

"Okay," he said disappointingly.

"What are your qualifications?" I asked.

"I know plumbing well. I worked on commercial buildings for years," he said.

He explained his work history. It amazed me. Martin was employed by a large, well-established plumbing company. His co-workers teased him often because he had a slight speech impediment. One day, his boss overheard the hurtful remarks.

"Martin," he said, waving Martin over to him. "Tomorrow, go directly to my house. Do not come here."

The next morning Martin went to his boss's house.

"I am going to teach you everything about plumbing," he said, putting his arm around Martin. "You will be a world-class plumber. Do not tell any of the other guys."

That man taught Martin how to be a world-class plumber and then some. When my first plumbing customer called me, I asked Martin to come along. His wealth of expertise was obvious. The moment my business grew, I increased his pay to forty dollars an hour. My therapist questioned the large increase.

"You are giving him forty?" she asked. "Why not twenty?"

"He really knows what he is doing," I said. "I cannot pay him medical or any other benefits. I want to pay him the most I can pay him. And I will learn from him."

When we started getting bigger jobs, I paid Martin fifty dollars an hour. Every day, I am thankful for him.

Business is good.

I am Jac, and these are my diaries.

A MAN'S WORLD

In case you have not noticed, most plumbers are men. I am one of the only female plumbers in the world who owns her own company, and in a male-dominated industry, it is not easy. While most tenants treat me like a million bucks, some of my male colleagues treat me like dirt.

Shortly after I took over the plumbing jobs for my building, the owner was so impressed with my skills, he asked me to work on his construction team. He wanted me to do plumbing and carpentry work for other buildings in the area. One of his managers, Jim, hated working alongside a woman. During one of our first jobs, he stole all my parts. What a jerk!

Another time, Jim and his buddies assigned me a job, hoping I would fail. Their goal was to make a laughingstock out of me. A woman had called numerous times during the past two years.

"My kids are cutting their feet," she said anxiously. "I have been calling for two years, asking for someone to come over and fix these six sharp nails poking out of my carpet. I hope you can fix it."

"I will be right over," I said, disgusted that it took two years for anyone to respond to the woman.

Her kids were young, about three and five-years-old. How could anyone have the audacity not to respond? One of the carpenters on Jim's team was working in a house next door. He could have easily gone into the woman's house and fixed the nails himself. Again, what jerks!

I pulled up to the apartment building. It was a stucco, two-story building with three units on the top and bottom. When I knocked on the door, the woman answered. She had shoulder-length, brown hair, and was about thirty years old.

"My kids are cutting their feet. No one would come out. I hope you can fix it. Please tell me you can fix it," she pleaded.

"I will figure this out," I said.

While I had no idea what to do and lacked carpentry experience, I was determined to learn how to fix the problem.

"Follow me," she said.

She led me through the house, repeatedly thanking me for showing up. I appreciated her sincerity and honesty.

We stopped in the living room. She pointed to the dark brown, shaggy carpet. It was old with rough, sharp edges.

"You have no idea," she said, turning towards me as if she was going to hug me. "I cannot believe you are here. It took me two years to get someone to help. Thank you so much."

She walked me to the spot where the carpet merged with the kitchen floor. Six, sharp nails stuck out from underneath.

"I tried pushing them down myself; however I could not do it," she explained.

I could see that pushing them down or knocking them over would not do the trick.

"I will be back today," I said.

I drove to a nearby hardware store to buy tools. Some hardware stores are a nightmare to visit. The employees treat me like dog meat because I am a woman. This store, however, always treated me like any other plumber – with respect.

A bell hanging from the front door announced my entrance.

"Hello Jac," said Jimmy, an older gentleman who worked at the store.

"Hi Jimmy," I said warmly. "I have a job that needs to get done today, and I have no idea how to do it."

I told him about the nails, and that none of the other carpenters responded to the woman's calls.

"For God's sake," he said. "I cannot believe no one helped her. That is terrible. You will fix it. I will tell you what to do."

Jimmy spent the next hour and a half teaching me, step-by-step, how to cover the nails. He showed me which tools to use and how and when to use them. I was so grateful.

"Thank you so much, Jimmy. I will let you know how it goes," I said.

I returned to the woman's house with my head held high. I knew how to fix the problem, and I was not leaving until I did it.

"I am back," I said.

"Thank you!" she exclaimed with relief.

I went to the living room and got to work. First, I cut the metal stripping to the exact size from the side wall to the front wall. Then, I laid it down and marked holes to fit the screws. I pulled back the strip, broke the cement where I marked the holes, and used my cordless screwdriver to insert the screws. The metal stripping covered the nails. The entire job took one hour.

I stepped back, admiring my work.

"That is it?" yelled the woman in disbelief.

"That is it!" I exclaimed.

"It took me two years to get someone to come over here, and you came and fixed it in one hour!" she said, overjoyed. "Thank you so much!"

Proudly, I walked outside to pack up my truck. A senior-level carpenter, who was working on the house next door, saw me.

"Where are you going?" he growled. "You have a job to do in there."

"I am done," I stated.

"Done? What?" he said, shocked a "girl" could finish the job so quickly.

"Yes, I am done. Finished," I gloated.

Carrying all his tools, he went to the woman's house to see it for himself. When he saw my fix, his tools dropped to the floor. His head dropped halfway to his knees. He could not believe it.

"Do you have something else you need me to do?" I asked smirking.

He was speechless. I got into my van and drove back to the shop.

Unfortunately, that job was not the first nor last time someone doubted my skills because of my gender. Nearly three years ago, I was on a lunch break at a restaurant in downtown Oakland. I liked stopping by the place between jobs. They served ribs, greens, and a couple pieces of crappy bread, which I never ate.

On that day, the restaurant was almost empty. After I finished eating, I had to use the bathroom. I walked up to the hostess stand to get the key.

"I need to use the bathroom," I said to the hostess. "May I have the key?"

"I am sorry," she said. "The bathroom is out of order."

"What is the matter with it?" I asked.

"The toilet will not flush," she said. "We have called several plumbers. No one can fix it."

Challenge accepted.

"May I take a look?" I asked.

She had a skeptical look on her face as if she was thinking, "Why would this random lady want to look at our toilet?"

"I am a plumber," I said. "My truck is out there. You can see my plumbing company's name on it."

"Well, the owner has been out here," she replied. "Plumbers were here too. No one can fix it."

"Can I look at it?" I asked again. "If I can fix it, I can use it, right?"

She smiled and handed me the key. I walked through the dining area to the bathroom. It was a large, single-stall room. The floor, sink, and walls were white. Nothing from the toilet had spilled onto the floor. For the most part, the room was clean. I assessed the toilet. Sure enough, it would not flush. I walked back to the hostess.

"Can I look in the kitchen?" I asked.

She seemed surprised.

"Let me check," she said and walked back into the kitchen to speak with the head chef.

I watched the two women through the circular window on the kitchen door. The chef nodded her head up and down. The hostess popped out her head from behind the swinging door.

"Sure, you can come in," she said, waving me over to her.

The kitchen smelled like smoky barbeque ribs. Pots and pans clanked loudly. Cooks were shouting orders. I spotted two large garbage bins against the side wall.

"How often are those garbage bins there? Do you move them at all?" I asked the chef.

"We move them around sometimes," she replied.

"Do you mind if I move them?" I asked.

She looked at me as if I had three eyes but gave me the go-ahead. I moved the bins to the right, which uncovered a vent.

"You see this vent right here?" I said to the chef and hostess, who were standing at full attention, wondering what the hell I was doing.

"Yes," they said in unison.

"That is the air vent to the toilet line," I said. "The bins were blocking the vent. Go into the bathroom now. I bet the toilet will flush. Actually, I will go with you."

The three of us went into the bathroom. The hostess flushed the toilet.

"Woosh!" It roared, flushing perfectly.

"Watch this," I said while putting a bunch of toilet paper into the bowl. "Now flush."

The hostess flushed it again.

"Woosh!" The toilet sucked everything down. The women looked amazed.

"Here is my card," I said. "Tell the owner to call me."

He never called. I went back to the restaurant a couple days later. The hostess seemed relieved to see me.

"It is blocked up again," she said.

I walked into the kitchen, saw the bins sitting in front of the vent and moved them.

"Woosh!" The toilet came to life.

"Why didn't the owner call me?" I asked the hostess.

"I showed him your card," she explained. "When he saw you were a woman, he did not believe anything you said."

Her eyes shifted downward to the floor.

"What a jackass!" I exclaimed. "He can go without a working toilet then."

The hostess looked ashamed or embarrassed. I could not tell. Either way, it was not her fault.

"How much do we owe you?" she asked quietly.

"Nothing," I said. "Do not worry about it."

Even though I despised the owner, I did not want the hostess to bear the brunt of his despicable behavior.

"Wait!" she yelled as I was walking out. "Do not leave yet. Sit down here."

She pointed to a low, two-top table.

A few minutes later, she brought me a big plate of ribs, greens, and the crappy bread, which I did not eat.

That meal was my last one at that restaurant.

THE BULL-HEADED BASTARD

Some men get excited when they discover I am a plumber. They see my truck pull up with my company's name on the side and joke that it should be called, "Women's Vagina Repair." They think it is hilarious. One time, when I was pulling out of a parking lot, two men and two women who were standing on the sidewalk pointed at my truck and laughed at me. I rolled down my window.

"That is right!" I yelled. "I am laughing all the way to the bank!"

That kind of stuff does not bother me. What does bother me, however, is when men underestimate my skills and assume they know more than me. One time an older man called me about a kitchen sink in his home.

"My kitchen sink is blocked," he said. "I tried unblocking it myself but cannot get it done."

"I will be right over," I said.

The man and his wife lived in the hills of Oakland. Their house was beautiful – white stucco with a brown trim and roof. It was a long, ranch house, with big windows and a two-car garage at the end. I parked in the driveway and knocked on the door. The wife answered.

"Hello. I am Jac, the plumber," I said.

"Hello," she responded, in a soft-spoken voice.

She looked like a schoolteacher. She had white hair and wore a small greenish-gray sweater on top of a white blouse and beige pants. She led me into the kitchen. Her husband was sitting at a round, wooden table, reading a newspaper, and drinking his morning coffee. He had a stern expression on his face.

"Hello. I am Bob," he said, standing up to greet me.

He wore professional clothing – khakis and a collared shirt. The kitchen was spotless, like my parents' kitchen. The plugged sink was on an island in the middle of the room.

"Can you show me where the pipes go?" I asked.

Bob pointed to the pipe, which ran from the kitchen sink, into the wall and over into the garage. It was a long pipe, about forty feet. He and his wife showed me the garage. It was beautiful. A newly lacquered, dark brown wooden coffee table stood in the center. Piles of fresh wood were stacked along the left side wall. Woodworking tools were on the right.

"Bob is a beautiful woodworker," beamed his wife.

The table was gorgeous.

"I need to look at the kitchen sink," I said.

I went back into the kitchen. Bob watched my every move, progressively pushing his newspaper further down from his eyes. I ran my snake down the sink into the pipe. When I yanked it back up, it was covered in thick, black, tar-like sludge. The snake went through several feet of sludge, yet it still did not pull out whatever was plugging the line. I suspected there was a restriction in the airline, which required me to open a cleanout under the sink.

"I need to open this cleanout," I told Bob.

"No. You are not going to do that," he stated defiantly. "We already tried that. That is not the problem."

"You did not tell me you tried that, although that is the problem," I replied. "I am going to open it anyway because there is a restriction in here. My snake is going through the sludge; however it is not unplugging the blockage. I need air."

"Do not open it," snapped Bob.

I bet you dollars to donuts he was an engineer.

"Fine," I said. "Then, I need to cut the pipe in the garage."

With Bob trailing my every step, I returned to the garage to assess the pipes. My snake peeked out of one of them, which meant it was going through the pipe without any blockage. In preparation for cutting the pipe, I grabbed my bucket and placed it underneath. That way if any sludge came out, it would fall into the bucket instead of onto the floor. Bob hastily moved my bucket and replaced it with his three-foot-wide bucket. To avoid confrontation, I moved my bucket slightly farther away in case any sludge splattered.

I cut the pipe. Sludge oozed out. I could see the pipe was packed with solid, black grease.

"This is what you are putting down your kitchen sink," I told Bob, showing him the grease.

He glanced at his wife, who sheepishly stood behind him.

It is extremely difficult to clear a line with grease. Once you poke a hole in it and pull the snake out, within seconds the grease packs in again. Thinking maybe the blockage was in that part of the pipe, I ran my snake down it. The pipe was loose enough for the snake to move back and forth, which meant that part was not the problem area.

"Maybe the problem is in the cleanouts outside," I thought.

I went outside to open the cleanouts, hoping the air would push the blockage out and into the buckets in the garage. I returned to the garage. Someone had moved my buckets.

"Who moved my buckets?" I yelled although I knew exactly who did it.

Bob did not understand how to deal with grease. Once I could get the air going, I knew the grub in the pipe would blow. I moved the buckets back to their original spots and went back outside to open the cleanouts.

When I returned to the garage, the buckets had been moved again.

"Who keeps moving my buckets?" I yelled again. "Leave them where I put them!"

I went back outside. When I returned to the garage, the buckets had been moved again.

"That is it!" I yelled irritated.

I moved the buckets one more time and went back into the kitchen. Bob snarled at me, perturbed it was taking so long to fix the problem.

"I am opening this cleanout," I said, pointing to the cleanout under the sink.

Little did I know, when I turned around, Bob, the control queen, raced back into the garage and moved the buckets one final time. I opened the cleanout.

"Whooooosh! Boom!" A rush of sludge burst out of the pipe, flying through the garage. It was like a fire hydrant opening, although instead of water gushing out, it was black muck.

"Oh my gosh," I thought. "I hope I caught it all in both buckets."

I went into the garage. Bob and his wife briskly followed me. Sludge was everywhere. It covered most of the wood and splattered on the lacquered coffee table. Some of it landed in my bucket. If Bob the bozo had not moved it, the bucket would have caught more.

"Who moved that bucket?" I asked Bob.

His wife stood behind him, looking perplexed, upset, and terrified. She slowly pointed to her husband. I wanted to call him a butthead, among many other names, yet I could not react. I had to maintain my professional demeanor.

"Why did you move that bucket?" I asked through clenched teeth. "I asked you three times not to move it. I told you the sludge would blow out."

"I did not believe you," he muttered.

My anger bubbled up more. If I were a man, I know he would have left my buckets alone.

Bob wanted to go off on me. I could see it in his eyes. Yet, he knew he was wrong.

"I wonder who will clean this up," I said.

There was no way I was going to do it.

"I will take care of it," he said.

His eyes remained glued to the mess.

Men always try to pull that controlling kind of bull shit. Bob paid the price for it.

THE WEMON

Plumbers find all kinds of things in toilets. One of my friends once found a light bulb in a bowl. She tried snaking it, then plunging it, however every time she thought she snagged it, the bulb rolled back. In a last-ditch effort, she placed the toilet bowl in the front yard and blew out the bulb with a hose.

I have certainly discovered my fair share of strange things. For example, on a warm, summer day, a woman called about a plugged toilet. She and her girlfriend owned a home daycare.

"I have a blocked toilet, Jac," she said. "It is the only toilet in the children's center, so we need it unplugged as soon as possible. Can you please come?" she pleaded.

"I will be right there," I replied.

Whenever I hear about women and children struggling with plugged toilets, lines, or anything else, I jump to the rescue. Besides, I knew the women well. In addition to the childcare center and main house, they also owned an apartment building and a spiritual gym. I was their go-to plumber for all those properties. One time, one of their tenants lost a fork down his toilet. I pulled it out.

The childcare center was in a back-house cottage. The women rented out the front house and lived in the cottage. A large, grassy yard sat between the two properties. It was filled with bouncy balls, toy houses, a swing set, and other colorful children's toys. The cottage looked like a large, brown bungalow. I knocked on the door. One of the women answered. She had short, red hair and a fair complexion. She wore typical summer clothes – long, beige shorts and a white collared, short-sleeve shirt.

"Thank you so much for coming so quickly, Jac," she said with a smile.

I always appreciated how grateful the women were whenever I came to help them.

"You are welcome, of course," I replied.

I walked inside. A large, carpeted living room was to the right of the entryway. It served as the napping and art space and had long rectangular, blue wooden tables with matching chairs scattered throughout the room. Colorful stickers and artwork adorned the walls. Kids were everywhere – drawing, playing tag, flying paper airplanes, and dancing. A little boy ran up to me.

"Hewo," he said, wrapping his arms around my leg.

"Hello there, little man," I said, holding out my hand for a high-five.

The woman led me past the kitchen to the bathroom. Reds, blues and yellows filled the space. A rainbow-colored stool stood in front of the sink. Toys piled in the bathtub. I could see someone had messed with the pipe in the bathroom wall. It looked bent and stuck out further than pipes usually do. The woman pointed to the plugged toilet. Only water sat in the bowl. Everything – from the toilet to the sink to the tub to the floor – was pristinely clean.

"This is the backed-up toilet," said the woman. "I will leave you to get to it."

I started with a plunger. There is a trick to plunging if you have the right one. It involves leveraging the weight of the water on top of the plunger. First, you must take off the lid of the tank. That way if the water begins to overflow when you flush, you can easily access the flapper to shut down the water. Then, you push the plunger down tightly into the bowl, repeatedly pump it up and down to get the air out while flushing at the same time, and pop it back forcefully. Usually, that method knocks out the blockage immediately. In this case, however, it was not successful. I tried running an auger down the bowl, which did not work either. I walked back into the living room to talk to the woman.

"Hey, something is really stuck in your toilet. It would be good to know what it is because I want to snag a piece and pull it out," I said.

I used that technique on a doll one time. It was stuck in the toilet, so I snagged a piece of its hair with my auger and pop! It came right out.

"I will do some investigating," said the woman.

I watched her approach a kid, gently asking if he put anything down the toilet. He shook his head from side to side. While she continued the investigation, I returned to the bathroom.

Within minutes, the woman followed.

"Jac," she said, standing in the doorway. Her hands rested on the shoulders of a little boy. He must have been about four years old.

"Matthew, tell Jac what you put down the toilet," she said calmly.

The poor kid looked scared. He fixated his eyes on the tile floor. His arms dangled at his sides.

"Matthew," I said gently. "Did you put something down this toilet?"

"I put down a wemon," he confessed.

"You put a lemon in here?" I asked.

He nodded his head up and down.

"Oh my gosh! We cannot get a lemon out!" I exclaimed playfully.

He did not seem to understand I was joking. His face scrunched slightly.

"It is okay, Matthew," I said, smiling. "You will never put a lemon down the toilet again, right? Because now I have to take off the whole toilet to get it out."

He nodded.

"You promise you will not do it again?" I asked. "Because this one time I will give them a break on the cost."

His eyes lit up. A slight smile emerged on his face. We all started giggling.

The woman escorted the boy back into the living room.

I removed the toilet, emptied the tank, and hauled it outside. Carrying a porcelain toilet can be dangerous. A while ago, I dropped one. It nearly sliced off my finger.

I carefully placed down the toilet on a patch of grass under a tree. The women took the children outside to play so they could help me while keeping an eye on them. Although it did not really matter. Most of the kids crowded around me, anyway, fascinated by the toilet and what I was about to do.

I stacked several coolers and placed the toilet on top.

"Please, tilt it down so I can see inside," I said to one of the women. "Do not move. Everyone do not move."

I felt like a doctor in an operating room. The kids' eyes remained glued on my every move.

First, I stuck a hose down the bowl. Every time I got close to the lemon, it rolled forward.

"I need a fork and knife, please," I said to the women. The redhead raced to the cottage. Within minutes she was back with a fork and knife in-hand. Clutching the knife, I speared the lemon and tried pulling it out, unsuccessfully.

"Oh!" yelled the crowd. "So close!"

I stuck the auger down again. It still would not penetrate the lemon.

"Can I help?" asked a little girl. "I can stick my hand in there."

"What a kind offer," I replied, crouching down in front of her. "But you see that down there?" I pointed to the hole at the bottom of the toilet. "That is the bottom of a toilet that you and your friends used."

The little girl slowly backed away.

"There is only one way left," I stated.

"Jac! Jac! Jac!" Everyone cheered.

Using the fork, I held down the lemon. Using the knife, I cut it into pieces.

"Go, Jac, go!" they continued cheering.

Fueled with determination, I shoved my hand down the hole and pulled out every piece of the lemon.

"Do you want this lemon back?" I said to Matthew, holding the soppy, wet chunks in the palm of my hand.

"Yeah, Jac! You did it!" Everyone cheered, clapping loudly and jumping up and down.

I felt like a superhero. Matthew screamed with excitement.

"You got the wemon!" he yelled, jumping up and down.

"Will you charge his parents for this?" I whispered to the women.

"We will tell them what happened," replied the redhead, smiling.

We all laughed. The kids returned to playing in the yard. I carried the toilet back inside, re-installed it and made sure it worked properly. I also fixed the bent pipe in the wall, which took two more hours; however I did not mind. Those cheering kids made my day.

DR. JACKYLL AND MR. HYDE

I am disabled. I do not have a meniscus in my left knee, so I cannot bend it. For the most part, I do not allow it to get in the way. I fix everything, no matter how challenging it may be for my body. One Sunday morning around 8 a.m., a young man named Eduardo called me. He and his father were hired to do landscape gardening in the front yard of a home.

"You need to come over here, quickly!" yelled Eduardo hysterically. "We hit a copper pipe with our pitch shovel! Water is spraying everywhere! We cannot stop it! Please, help!"

"Did you call the city?" I asked.

Usually, when a worker pops a hole in a pipe underground, the city comes out to turn off the water.

"We did," he said. "They have not come yet. They said it would take three hours!"

"I am not feeling well," I said. "And, on Sundays, I charge two hundred dollars an hour."

I truly felt awful. My entire body ached, and I had a raging headache. Before Eduardo called, I had planned to stay in bed all morning.

"That is okay," he said. "The homeowners will pay your rate. Please, please, can you come?"

"Ugh, okay," I groaned, swinging my legs out of bed. "Although I am only turning off the water. I am not fixing the pipe."

The house was in the wealthy part of Oakland. Every block had sprawling homes with perfectly manicured lawns. In front of a large, gray, brick home, I saw two men walking intensely back and forth across a dug up front yard that was drowning in water.

"That must be it," I said to myself.

I pulled into the driveway. Fresh trees lined the blacktop. Flowers were halfway planted in the sopping ground. The yard was a pool of slushy mud.

"What a mess," I said, getting out of my truck.

It was obvious where Eduardo and his father hit the pipe. Water sprayed out of it like the Niagara Falls.

"Did you turn off the water?" I asked Eduardo. "Do you have the key?"

Shutting off the water required using an iron key to unlock a panel in the street. City crews typically have the key. Trade workers sometimes receive one too if they are working on a job nearby.

"Yes, we have the key," said Eduardo.

"So, why didn't you use it?" I asked dumbfounded.

"I could not get it open," he replied.

"You could not get it open?" I repeated.

Eduardo had muscles coming out of his ears. How could he not turn the key?

I hurriedly grabbed the key, walked over to the panel, and turned off the water in seconds.

"Are you kidding me?" I yelled, staring at Eduardo. He shrugged his shoulders.

The homeowners, who were a husband and wife, were standing outside the front door, watching us run back and forth. The husband had brownish-gray, short hair and wore dark jeans and a white t-shirt. The wife had long, brown hair and wore an ankle-length, bright yellow skirt and a white t-shirt.

"I am Jack," said the husband, extending his arm to shake my hand. "Did you shut off the water?"

"It is off," I said.

He and his wife were thrilled.

"Thank you so much!" they exclaimed.

"That will be two hundred bucks," I said.

"Actually," said Jack. "Can you please fix the pipe too? We will pay you."

Fixing the pipe involved cutting a foot of copper. I would have needed to go to the hardware store, buy another piece of copper pipe, and return to install it. Considering I already felt like garbage, I did not want to overtax my body. I dreamed about crawling back into bed.

"Look," I said. "I am sorry. I do not feel well and have a bum knee. I really cannot do this today."

Around the side of the house, I heard a child laughing.

"That is our son," said the wife. "He is four-years-old. We need the water on for tonight. We cannot go a full day without water."

"I can send a guy over tomorrow morning, first thing, to fix it," I said.

"Please!" she pleaded. "We cannot find anyone who can come out on a Sunday. We tried. We cannot even get the city to come out!"

"Yes, I know it is tough," I said. "But I told your landscaper that I would only shut off the water. He said you agreed, and you would pay me two hundred dollars."

"That is true," said Jack. "But is there any way you can consider fixing the pipe too? We have a child!"

Again, my soft spot for children prevailed.

"Oh, okay. I will do it," I said.

The couple was so ecstatic I thought they might hug me. I went to the store, bought the copper pipe, and returned. Eduardo and his father were running around like chickens with their heads cut off.

"Hey!" I yelled at them. "Can you please dig up this ground so I can access the pipe?"

They grabbed their shovels and dug a hole around the side of the pipe. It was made of soft copper, which moves a lot. Fixing and installing a soft copper pipe perfectly straight into the ground is significantly more difficult than if it were hard copper. Not to mention, I still was not feeling well. Hobbling around and slipping on mud, I went back to my truck to grab a tarp. When I returned to the hole, a city truck pulled up next to the curb. A slim, friendly-looking man stepped out.

"Hi there," he said. "I am Doug. I work for the city. I see the water is shut off. You did that?"

"I did," I replied.

"Way to go!" he exclaimed. "Those big guys could not get it off!"

Embarrassed, Eduardo and his father looked down at the ground. I hobbled over to Doug's truck.

"Here is the deal," I said softly. "I have a bum knee and do not feel well. I will give you one hundred bucks if you fix that pipe. You have good knees. I will pay you."

"I am sorry, ma'am," he replied. "I work for the city. It is illegal for me to do a job like that. I wish I could help."

Disappointed, I hobbled back to the hole and began prepping the pipe. First, I cleaned off the mud. Then, I sanded it down and cut it. I collected the other pieces and sanded them down too. I needed to lower my body inside the hole to connect the pieces underground, however, because I could not bend my right knee, it was nearly impossible.

Doug saw me struggling and walked over to the hole. "Alright," he said, feeling sorry for me. "I will do it."

"Thank you so much," I replied, relieved.

He lowered himself into the hole while I stood next to him to assist. Jack and his wife stood near us, watching our every move.

Because of the soft copper, it took more than an hour for Doug and me to put it back into the ground. Every now and then, Jack and his wife would step back to talk amongst themselves. They whispered to each other while glancing in our direction. They could see I was not the one inside the hole; however I was helping Doug with every step.

At first, we did not think the pipe took. When you work with copper, you cannot have any dirt clinging to the pipe. Both ends must be perfectly round. Doug became frustrated with me because I kept insisting the pipe did not take. He lowered himself back into the hole and pulled it upwards. The whole thing moved as one, solid pipe.

"Is this good enough?" he asked. "That is solid. Let's turn the water back on."

"Listen, you can go," I said anxiously.

Doug was losing patience, and I did not want him to get in trouble for helping me. His boss must have been wondering why he was not back in the office an hour ago.

"I can turn the water back on by myself. Thank you for your help," I said.

"Okay," he said and left.

Before turning the water on at the street level, I had to let the air escape from inside the house. Still not feeling well, I hobbled around the side of the house to open the hose bibs. I then went inside the home to make sure the faucets were turned off. The child's nanny stood at the kitchen counter with a scowl on her face.

"Why are you bossing everyone around?" she snapped.

"I am the plumber, ma'am," I said, trying not to explode. "Your boss begged me to fix the pipe and get the water turned on, so that is what I am doing. Did anyone open a faucet or flush a toilet in the past two hours?"

She turned her back to me, looking outside the kitchen window. "What do you mean by 'open?'" she asked.

"I mean did you flush any toilets or turn on any faucets?" I replied.

"I turned on the faucet upstairs," she said curtly.

I ran upstairs, removed the aerator attached to the end of the faucet, and went back downstairs. Eduardo was standing in the kitchen.

"Listen," I said. "I am turning on the water. You stay down here and aim the hose into the kitchen sink."

The nanny rolled her eyes and stormed out. She was pissed. She did not approve of me throwing orders around.

"I am trying to get the water on!" I yelled as she left.

I approached Jack and his wife.

"I am sorry your nanny is pissed at me," I explained. "I do not mean to be bossy; I just want to get the water back on. Please do not close the hose bibs. We need them open to let the air run through."

They looked at me like I had two heads. They had no idea what I was saying. Frustrated, I walked away to go turn on the water. Everything worked perfectly, thank goodness. Between the rude nanny, soft copper piping, my bum leg, poor health, the muddy ground, and oblivious homeowners, my patience was wearing thin. I walked back inside the house to talk to Jack and his wife.

"It is fixed. The water is on and working fine," I said. "If you can pay me, I would appreciate it."

"Well," said Jack. "You had some help."

A flash of anger rushed through my body.

"You saw me hobbling around. I told you I was not feeling well. So, yes, I got help," I said, trying everything in my power to keep my cool. "The pipe was several feet underground. Because of my bum knee, I literally had to lay down on the tarp to reach down there."

"That guy did all the work," he retorted.

"I turned off your water and turned it back on. I helped him during the entire job. I have been here for more than two hours. You owe me $400 plus $56 for the parts. Considering it is a Sunday, you got a good deal," I said, mustering every ounce of patience in my body.

Jack handed me a check.

"Thank you," I said. "And listen, please do not say anything to the city. That guy was not supposed to help me. He could get in trouble if you tell on him."

"Okay, thanks," he replied.

We shook hands, and I left.

I assumed everything ended on a positive note. I went out of my way to fix their pipe and turn on the water, despite feeling like garbage and hobbling around with a bum knee. A few days later, however, I realized I was wrong.

I regularly peruse my customer reviews online. All of them were positive until Jack wrote one that was scathing. He accused me of bossing everyone around, complaining about my "ailments," and charging $450 even though someone helped me. His public remarks shocked me to my core.

I replied instantly, reminding Jack that he and his wife begged me to fix their pipe. I emphasized that they thanked me profusely for agreeing to help. I also wished them nothing but the best.

Jack's wife replied with another review. She called me "untruthful." She claimed I never said I was not feeling well, which was not true. She also said she was disappointed in my "business ethics."

I was horrified. They were the most two-faced people I had ever met. In-person, they praised me. Online, they shamed me, and it hurt my business. Before they wrote those reviews, I was receiving twenty to thirty calls a day. After those reviews were posted, I received maybe three calls a day. Just one customer truly has the power to damage my business, and my business is everything to me. I have not had a lover in years. My dad, who was an abusive alcoholic, died. My brother recently passed away from an environmental illness. My other two brothers are alcoholics. I do not have any family. My business is all I have in this world, and for someone to trash me publicly like that, after I went out of my way to help them, was heartbreaking.

A MOMENT OF REFLECTION

I am so grateful for my plumbing skills. The education and experience have been a blessing. I love most of my customers. Some of them have even become my friends. About a month ago, I went to a woman's house to shut off her water. She could not get the city to come out and do it. I did not charge her. The job took ten minutes. In a couple months, I am having surgery. That same woman offered to help me during my recovery. She and so many other customers go above and beyond to show their gratitude.

Everywhere I go, people in the streets approach me, asking how I am doing. In my own apartment building, I am treated like a celebrity. I have helped many of the tenants at no cost. One time, a guy on the fourth floor was hosting a Superbowl party. He had six friends coming over to watch the game. Before they arrived, he knocked on my door in a panic.

"Jac, the building owner told me a plumber was supposed to come fix my clogged kitchen sink," he said. "The plumber did not show up. I have all these people coming over, and plates piled high to the ceiling. Can you please help?"

"Sure, give me a minute," I replied.

The guy was so nice. Of course, I was going to help him. I went to his apartment to assess the situation.

Dirty dishwater pooled in the sink. Underneath, the whole drain was rusted out. His buddies arrived shortly after me. They tried helping me remove the rusty drain. Each one flipped over on his back, shimmied his way under the sink, and tried yanking it off. The drain would not budge.

"Alright," I said after the fifth guy tried unsuccessfully. "Everyone out of the kitchen. I will do this."

Finally, after using almost every tool in my bag, I pulled it off. The project took an hour. The guy was so grateful, he left a pot of jambalaya and a two-page, glowing review at my door. The review, which he typed and printed on crisp, white paper, explained in detail that no one showed up to help him except for me and that anyone who hired me would be doing their company a great service. I read the review three times, feeling like I was in seventh heaven.

Of course, not everyone was as sweet as that guy. I have faced my fair share of sexism and classism. People have looked down on me because I am working class, yet when they are in trouble and need my services, they change their tune.

Over time, I have learned to filter out the crazies. After being clean and sober for thirty-two years, I can spot someone who uses drugs, drinks excessively, or is off-kilter. When those kinds of people call, I politely turn them down. I also steer clear of people who hem and haw about the price for my services. They will call me to fix a plugged sink or install a hot water heater. During our first conversation, I will tell them the price.

"Well," they will say hesitantly. "Why don't you just come out and we will talk about the money then?"

"Actually, I prefer to talk about the money now," I will reply. I then courteously tell them that I need to hang up.

Today, I am choosier about jobs. Many people call me, emphasizing they only want me to do the job. One woman called yesterday about a leaking bathtub faucet and garbage disposal, and a slow-to-drain tub.

"Jac, don't worry," she said. "Whatever you charge, we will pay. We only want you."

Well, how can I say "no" to that?

THE END

*If you are a contractor of any kind and have interesting,
funny, and/or memorable stories to share,
please contact me at
abbynews@hotmail.com
or message me on Twitter at @HonestAb2*

NOTE FROM THE AUTHOR

Word-of-mouth is crucial for any author to succeed. If you enjoyed the book, please leave a review online—anywhere you are able. Even if it's just a sentence or two. It would make all the difference and would be very much appreciated.

Thanks!
Abby

ABOUT THE AUTHOR

Abby Ross has nearly two decades of experience working in journalism, public relations, and marketing. She has written countless news stories, bylines, and blog posts. Abby began her career as a television news reporter, which fostered her passion for interviewing and writing about interesting people from all walks of life. After six years of reporting, Abby pivoted her career into public relations and marketing, which has been her focus for the past decade. This is her first book.

Facebook – https://www.facebook.com/abby.rosstoth
Twitter – @honestab2
Instagram – @honestab2
LinkedIn – https://www.linkedin.com/in/abby-ross

Thank you so much for reading
one of our **Humor** novels.

If you enjoyed our book,
please check out our recommendation
for your next great read!

Parrot Talk by David B. Seaburn

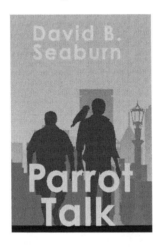

"...a story of abandonment, addiction, finding oneself—
all mixed in with tear-jerking chapters next to laugh-
out-loud chapters." –*Tiff & Rich*

Made in the USA
Middletown, DE
07 April 2022